Pocket
HOBART
TOP SIGHTS • LOCAL LIFE • MADE EASY

WITHDRAWN

Charles Rawlings-Way

In This Book

QuickStart Guide

Your keys to understanding the city – we help you decide what to do and how to do it

Need to Know
Tips for a smooth trip

Neighbourhoods
What's where

Explore Hobart

The best things to see and do, neighbourhood by neighbourhood

Top Sights
Make the most of your visit

Local Life
The insider's city

The Best of Hobart

The city's highlights in handy lists to help you plan

Best Walks
See the city on foot

Hobart's Best...
The best experiences

Survival Guide

Tips and tricks for a seamless, hassle-free city experience

Arriving in Hobart
Travel like a local

Essential Information
Including where to stay

Our selection of the city's best places to eat, drink and experience:

◎ **Sights**

✖ **Eating**

🍷 **Drinking**

⭐ **Entertainment**

🛍 **Shopping**

These symbols give you the vital information for each listing:

☎	Telephone Numbers	👪	Family-Friendly
⊙	Opening Hours	🐾	Pet-Friendly
P	Parking	🚌	Bus
⊖	Nonsmoking	⛴	Ferry
@	Internet Access	Ⓜ	Metro
🛜	Wi-Fi Access	Ⓢ	Subway
🥗	Vegetarian Selection	🚋	Tram
📖	English-Language Menu	🚆	Train

Find each listing quickly on maps for each neighbourhood:

Bar Hemingway

16 🍷 Map p233, B2

Legend has it that Hemi self, wielding a machine
rate this timber-pan
ered bar during
showpiece is a
en by Papa ar
town. Dress
s.com; Hôtel Rit
⊙ 6.30pm-2a

Lonely Planet's Hobart

Lonely Planet Pocket Guides are designed to get you straight to the heart of the city.

Inside you'll find all the must-see sights, plus tips to make your visit to each one really memorable. We've split the city into easy-to-navigate neighbourhoods and provided clear maps so you'll find your way around with ease. Our expert authors have searched out the best of the city: walks, food, nightlife and shopping, to name a few. Because you want to explore, our 'Local Life' pages will take you to some of the most exciting areas to experience the real Hobart.

And of course you'll find all the practical tips you need for a smooth trip: itineraries for short visits, how to get around, and how much to tip the guy who serves you a drink at the end of a long day's exploration.

It's your guarantee of a really great experience.

Our Promise

You can trust our travel information because Lonely Planet authors visit the places we write about, each and every edition. We never accept freebies for positive coverage, so you can rely on us to tell it like it is.

QuickStart Guide 7

Explore Hobart 23

Worth a Trip:

The Best of Hobart **123**

Hobart's Best Walks

Hobart's Best ...

Survival Guide **145**

QuickStart Guide

Welcome to Hobart

Backed by towering Kunanyi/Mt Wellington, Hobart is a harbour city where the world rushes in on the tide. Down on the waterfront, old pubs sit alongside new craft-beer bars, myriad restaurants, cafes, museums...all of it washed with sea-salty charm and a sense of history. MONA, Hobart's dizzyingly good Museum of Old and New Art, is just north of town.

Boats at Victoria Dock (p53)
CYRUS_2000 / SHUTTERSTOCK ©

Hobart
Top Sights

MONA/RÉMI CHAUVIN, IMAGE COURTESY MONA, MUSEUM OF OLD AND NEW ART, HOBART

MONA (p88)
Hobart's show-stopping Museum of Old & New Art is a force of culture.

Salamanca Place (p44)
The old stone warehouses are pretty as a picture. But what's inside them is the real lure.

TRAVELGAME / GETTY IMAGES ©

Battery Point (p94)

Hobart's first suburb, where 1800s cottages line tightly nested streets.

Kunanyi/Mt Wellington (p118)

The mountain that towers over Hobart like a benevolent overlord.

North Hobart (p72)

The city's bohemian heart- and art-land.

GRANT DIXON / GETTY IMAGES ©

RACHEL LEWIS / GETTY IMAGES ©

Cascade Brewery (p110)

Since 1832, the formula 'Hobart + beer = Cascade' has been an unshakable truth.

Tasmanian Museum & Art Gallery (p48)

'TMAG' houses Tasmania's most extensive collection of paintings and relics.

Cascades Female Factory Historic Site (p114)

Where Hobart's female convicts were incarcerated and put to work.

Hobart
Local Life

*Local experiences and hidden gems
to help you uncover the real city*

Hobart is compact, sandwiched between the mountain and the river, but that doesn't mean that it's an obvious sort of place. Some local know-how is required to access the city's history, charms, quirks and hidden corners.

City Centre Shuffle (p26)
☑ Shopping ☑ Hidden history

On the Waterfront (p52)

☑Docks, piers & warehouses ☑Seafood

North Hobart Streetwise (p76)

☑Eating & drinking ☑Entertainment

Battery Point Backstreets (p98)

☑ Historic sites ☑ Architecture

Other great places to experience the city like a local:

Street Eats @ Franko (p34)

Hope & Anchor (p47)

Flamingos Dance Bar (p38)

Salamanca Arts Centre Courtyard (p47)

Sydney to Hobart Yacht Race (p57)

University of Tasmania School of Art (p60)

Telegraph Hotel (p66)

Capulus Espresso (p82)

Raincheck Lounge (p85)

RICHARD I'ANSON / GETTY IMAGES ©

Hobart
Day Planner

Day One

Get your head into history mode with an amble around the storied precinct of **Battery Point** (p94). Don't miss the photogenic cottages around Arthur Circus and the Hampden Rd cafes, like **Jackman & McRoss** (p102).

After lunch, wander down Kelly's Steps to the historic warehouses on **Salamanca Place** (p44): check out the shops and galleries in the **Salamanca Arts Centre** (p56) and get caffeinated at **Tricycle Cafe & Bar** (p60). Delve into Hobart's Antarctic heritage at the **Mawson's Huts Replica Museum** (p56) over near Constitution Dock, before a fish-and-chip dinner at **Flippers** (p59) floating fish punt.

Afterwards, grab a drink at the upmarket **Glass House** (p63) in the floating Brooke Street Pier.

Day Two

On day two, recuperate over a big brunch and multiple coffees at **Retro Cafe** (p59) on Salamanca Place; if it's a Saturday, **Salamanca Market** (p66) will be pumping.

Afterwards, ferry out to **MONA** (p89) for an afternoon of mindful distraction in the museum's amazing subterranean galleries. Grab a drink at one of MONA's bars, then cab-it back to **North Hobart** (p72) for dinner at **Pancho Villa** (p81) or **Roaring Grill** (p84).

For a crafty brew after dinner, try the bohemian cool **Winston** (p84) or a glass of vino at **Willing Bros** (p85). See what's screening at the arthouse **State Cinema** (p86) or trundle down to the **Republic Bar & Café** (p86) for some live tunes.

Short on time?
We've arranged Hobart's must-sees into these day-by-day itineraries to make sure you see the very best of the city in the time you have available.

Day Three

☀ Have you noticed massive **Kunanyi/Mt Wellington** (p119) behind the city? Drive up Pinnacle Rd to the peak and scan the horizon, or mountain-bike down the slopes on the **Mt Wellington Descent** (p120). Grab lunch at **Ginger Brown** (p111) in South Hobart afterwards.

☀ At the foot of Mt Wellington are the **Cascade Brewery** (p111) and the **Cascades Female Factory Historic Site** (p115). Tour the ruins of the Female Factory convict prison first, then soothe your frayed nerves at Hobart's legendary brewery nearby.

☾ In the evening, settle in for some super Italian at **Don Camillo** (p107) in upmarket Sandy Bay (one of the city's oldest restaurants). Post-pasta drinks await back on buzzy Salamanca Place: try **Jack Greene** (p63) or **Waterman's Beer Market** (p64).

Day Four

☀ Take it downtown. Grab breakfast at hip **Pilgrim Coffee** (p35), then hit the shops: **Cool Wine** (p27) for some booze, **Tommy Gun Records** (p27) for some music, or the Sunday-morning **Farm Gate Market** (p34) for all things organic, local and edible.

☀ Backstreet **Templo** (p34) is a hit for lunch, then meander down to the outstanding **Tasmanian Museum & Art Gallery** (p48) near the waterfront for a shot of culture.

☾ Treat yourself to a top-flight South American dinner at **Frank** (p61), then wander over the laid-back **Hobart Brewing Company** (p63) to bend an elbow with the locals.

Need to Know

**For more information,
see Survival Guide (p145)**

Currency
Australian dollar ($)

Language
English

Visas
All visitors to Australia need a visa, except
New Zealanders. Apply online at
www.border.gov.au.

Money
The major banks all have branches and
ATMs around Elizabeth St Mall. There are
also ATMs around Salamanca Place.

Mobile Phones
European phones will work on Australia's
network, but most American or Japanese
phones will not. Use global roaming or buy a
local SIM card with a prepaid account.

Time
Australian Eastern Standard Time (AEST;
GMT/UCT plus 10 hours)

Plugs & Adaptors
Standard voltage is 240V/50Hz. Plugs
are either two or three pins. International
adaptors are widely available.

Tipping
Tipping in Australia is common in many
situations (eg restaurants – 10% is the norm)
but it certainly isn't mandatory.

① Before You Go

Your Daily Budget

Budget: Less than $150
► Double hostel room: $80–100
► Budget pizza or pasta meal: $15–20
► Local bus ride: from $3.30

Midrange: $150–300
► Double room in a motel or B&B: $130–250
► Cafe brunch: $20–30
► Short taxi ride: $25

Top End: More than $300
► Double boutique hotel room: from $250
► Classy three-course restaurant meal: $80
► MONA admission including ferry: $50

Useful Websites

Lonely Planet (www.lonelyplanet.com/
australia/tasmania/hobart) Destination
information, hotel bookings, traveller forum
and more.

Hobart & Beyond (www.hobartandbeyond.
com.au) Places to stay, things to do and
where to eat and drink.

Tasmanian Travel & Information Centre
(www.hobarttravelcentre.com.au) Hobart's
info and bookings hub.

Advance Planning

Three months before During summer,
Easter or June's Dark MOFO festival, book
beds and restaurants early.

One month before Book popular tours (Mt
Wellington Descent, Cascade Brewery, boat
trips) and MONA tickets.

One week before Check the weather
forecast: Hobart can sweat in November
then freeze in December.

2 Arriving in Hobart

✈ From Hobart Airport

Hobart's 'international' airport is at Cambridge, 19km east of the city. Many visitors to the city rent a car (there are many rental desks in the airport terminal). A taxi into the city will cost around $50 and take about 20 minutes. Pre-booked shuttle buses (adult/child $19/14) with Hobart Airporter (www.airporterhobart.com.au) meet every flight and deliver you to city hotels.

⛴ From Devonport Ferry Terminal

If you're arriving by ferry from Melbourne, the big red boat spits you out in Devonport on Tasmania's northwest coast. It's a 3¼-hour drive from here to Hobart.

3 Getting Around

🚗 Car & Motorcycle

The quickest way to get around. Competition keeps car-rental prices reasonable.

🚕 Taxi

Hop from venue to venue.

🏃 Walking

Explore the city centre, waterfront and Battery Point under your own steam.

🚲 Bicycle

Hobart is hilly but super-scenic from the seat of a bike.

🚌 Bus

Use Hobart's clean, affordable public transport if you must, but services can be infrequent, especially after dark and on weekends. See www.metrotas.com.au.

Hobart
Neighbourhoods

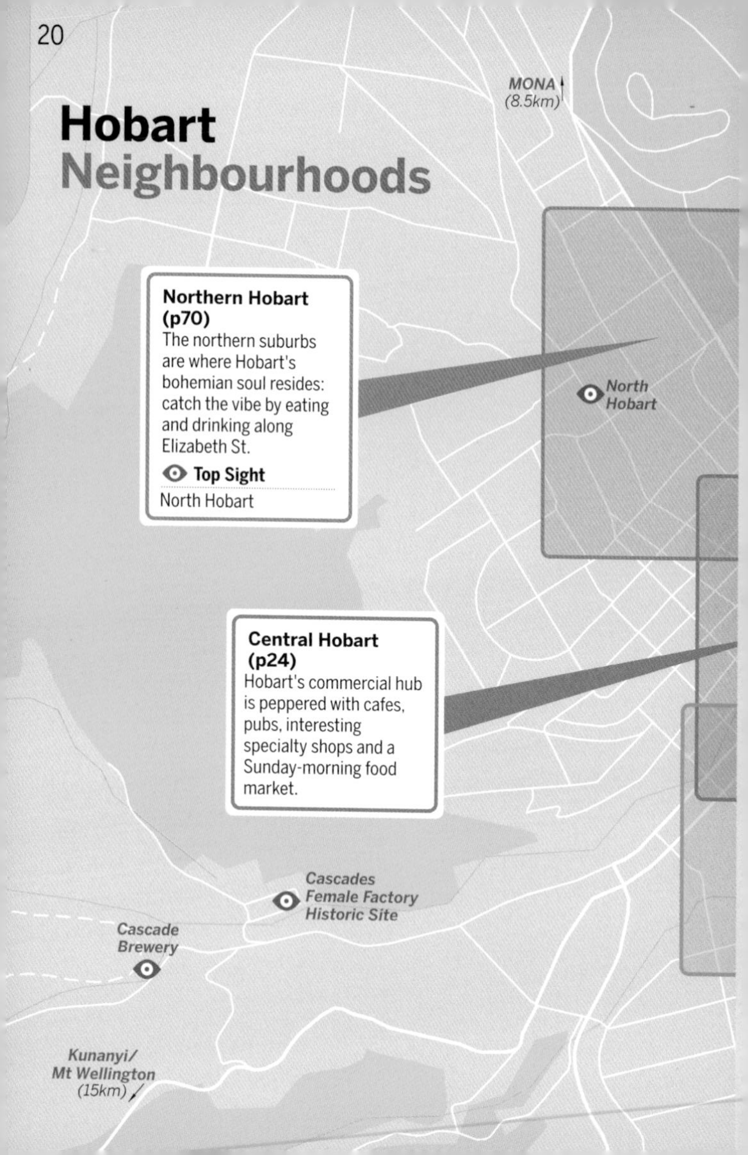

MONA
(8.5km)

Northern Hobart (p70)
The northern suburbs are where Hobart's bohemian soul resides: catch the vibe by eating and drinking along Elizabeth St.

◉ **Top Sight**
North Hobart

◉ North Hobart

Central Hobart (p24)
Hobart's commercial hub is peppered with cafes, pubs, interesting specialty shops and a Sunday-morning food market.

Cascades
Female Factory
◉ Historic Site

Cascade
Brewery
◉

Kunanyi/
Mt Wellington
(15km)

Worth a Trip

⊙ Top Sights

MONA (p88)

Cascade Brewery (p110)

Cascades Female Factory Historic Site (p114)

Kunanyi/Mt Wellington (p118)

MONA (9km)

Salamanca Place & the Waterfront (p42)

Salamanca's row of honey-hued 1830s sandstone former warehouses is the heart of Hobart's effervescent waterfront precinct.

⊙ Top Sights

Salamanca Market

Tasmanian Museum & Art Gallery

Battery Point, Sandy Bay & South Hobart (p92)

From the old whalers' cottages in Battery Point to affluent Sandy Bay and atmospheric South Hobart, these three suburbs shine a light on Hobart's history.

⊙ Top Sight

Battery Point

⊙ Tasmanian Museum & Art Gallery

⊙ Salamanca Place

⊙ Battery Point

Explore
Hobart

Worth a Trip

Light installation by artist Rafael Lozano-Hemmers during
Dark Mofo (p144)
STEVE LOVEGROVE / SHUTTERSTOCK ©

Explore

Central Hobart

Hobart's CBD is a long way from the high-rise architectural hedonism of the mainland Australian capitals. But among the stunted skyscrapers, Hobartians get busy with excellent cafes, endearing pubs, interesting shops and most of Hobart's budget accommodation. There are some top restaurants here, too, turning their backs on the more obvious glamour of the waterfront.

The Sights in a Day

 Start your downtown day with a serious coffee at **Pilgrim Coffee** (p35) – an enshrinement of Hobart hipsterism. Tourist sights in the city centre are more quirky than predictable: check out the amazing **Hobart Real Tennis Club** (p29), one of only three such courts in the southern hemisphere; or tour the **Theatre Royal** (p29; pictured), Australia's oldest working theatre. For lunch, pint-sized **Small Fry** (p35) is an appealing little nook.

 Just across Bathurst St is the brutal-looking State Library, home to the engaging **Allport Library & Museum of Fine Arts** (p30) – repository of all manner of curious old artworks, photos, books and antiques. Suck some more caffeine at **Yellow Bernard** (p34), then truck down to the **Gasworks Cellar Door** (p30) near the waterfront for a one-stop tour of Tasmania's wine regions.

☾ When evening descends, head to the **New Sydney Hotel** (p36) for a pre-dinner drink, then hit compact **Templo** (p34) for a some contemporary Hobart cooking. See who's playing at the **Brisbane Hotel** (p40) afterwards: could be anyone from an earnest singer-songwriter to an in-your-face punk outfit.

For a local's day in central Hobart, see p26.

○ Local Life

♥ Best of Hobart

Eating

Drinking

Shopping

Getting There

🚶 Walk Central Hobart is relatively flat and parking is limited – get around on foot.

🚌 Bus All bus routes lead to central Hobart: bus into the city then walk around once you're there.

🚕 Taxi If you're staying in Sandy Bay or somewhere further flung, grab a cab into the city.

Local Life
City Centre Shuffle

Downtown Hobart isn't what you'd call a buzzing metropolis. There are no canyons of commerce, skyscrapers or subterranean train networks here. Instead what you'll find is an endearing city centre offering up some excellent speciality shops and arcades, quality spots for a coffee and some curious corners where Hobart's history peeps through the modernity.

....

❶ **What Lies Beneath** Hobart's original water source, the **Hobart Rivulet** wiggles right through the middle of the CBD. In most places the rivulet has been built over, but on Molle St at the western edge of the city centre you can get a good look at it – still a lovely little rocky stream at this point, before it's banished into underground culverts.

② Centrepoint Arcade

A wiggly shopping arcade built over the top of the Hobart Rivulet, split-level Centrepoint Arcade came into being in the 1980s and remains somewhat mired in these inglorious architectural days. But the shops here are fab: enter off Victoria St and wander your way past boutiques, cafes, jewellers, a perfumery, deli, florist, bookshop, newsagent, travel store...

③ Cat & Fiddle Arcade

Cross Murray St, still following the course of the Hobart Rivulet hidden below, and explore Cat & Fiddle Arcade, a two-tier shopping enclave which opened in 1962. A classic Hobart kids' experience is to see the animated Cat & Fiddle Clock playing out its little pantomime hourly from 8am to 11pm: cow jumping moon, little dog laughing, dish and spoon absconding etc.

④ Mall Life

At the eastern end of Cat & Fiddle Arcade is the **Elizabeth St Mall** – a classic piece of erroneous 1980s town-planning that saw one of Hobart's busiest streets closed off to traffic. Still, it remains a busy shopping hub. Interestingly, an historic stone bridge over the rivulet was exposed during recent building works here: the resultant hole-in-the-mall now affords a rare window onto the chuckling rivulet below.

⑤ Fine Wine

One of Hobart's best speciality shops is **Cool Wine** (☎03 6231 4000; www.coolwine.com.au; shop 8, MidCity Arcade, Criterion St; ◎9.30am-6.30pm Mon-Sat), a neat little independent booze vendor in the MidCity Arcade. Duck inside and peruse its fab selection of cool-climate Tasmanian wines, beers and spirits (plus a few good ones from other places).

⑥ Cool Tunes

From cool wine to cool tunes: Hobart is a musical kinda town, and the best little record shop in the city is **Tommy Gun Records** (☎03 6234 2039; www.facebook.com/tommygunhobart; 127 Elizabeth St; ◎10am-5.30pm Mon-Fri, to 3pm Sat) on Elizabeth St. Stop by and check out the racks of vinyl (new and second-hand), plus bad-ass metal T-shirts and DJ tech.

⑦ Coffee on Criterion

Short and sweet Criterion St, between Liverpool and Bathurst Sts, has evolved in to a simmering coffee hub. **Criterion Street Café** (☎03 6234 5858; 10 Criterion St; mains $6-18; ◎7am-4pm Mon-Fri, 8am-3pm Sat & Sun) was the trailblazer here, with new hole-in-the-wall coffee nooks like **Ecru** (☎0448 738 014; www.ecrucoffee.com.au; 18 Criterion St; items from $3; ◎7am-3pm Mon-Fri, 8.30am-12.30pm Sun) and **Villino** (☎03 6231 0890; www.villino.com.au; 30 Criterion St; items $5-12; ◎8am-4.30pm Mon-Fri, 9am-3pm Sat) popping up recently.

A

B

C

D

Patrick St

Brisbane St

Brooker Ave

Tasman Hwy

25

5
Penitentiary
Chapel
Historic Site

Campbell St

Railway
Roundabout

Brooker Ave

Elizabeth St

Tassielink

Melville St

Argyle St

Bathurst St

Hobart
Police
Station

Liverpool St

Theatre
Royal

1

Gasworks
Cellar Door

4

Evans St

21

22

16

Royal
Hobart
Hospital

Collins St

Campbell St

Macquarie St

Dunn Pl St

23 18

Murray St

12 11
Criterion St
3 24

Elizabeth St

Bank Arc

Elizabeth St Mall

20

Argyle St

Davey St

Victoria
Dock

17

Bathurst St

Allport Library
& Museum of
Fine Arts

Cat & Fiddle
Arc

The
Place

Hobart
Comedy
Tours 9

Elizabeth
St

10
Mawson
Place

Constitution
Dock

Kings
Pier
Marina

15

30

Watchorn St

14

26

Centrepoint
Arc

13

28

St David's
Cathedral

7

Murray St

Government
Offices

Hobart
Historic
Tours

Brooke St

Elizabeth St
Pier

Brooke St
Pier

Morrison St

Sullivans
Cove

Goulburn St

Harrington St

Victoria St

19

Hobart
Real Tennis
Club

2

Parks &
Wildlife
Service

Murray St

Parliament
House

Parliament
Square

Montpelier Rd

Princes
Wharf

Castray Esp

Liverpool St

Hobart
Airporter

27

Collins St

29

Redline
Coaches

Barrack St

Macquarie St

Davey St

Markree
House
Museum

6

Wilmot St

St David's
Park

Supreme
Court

Commonwealth
Law Courts

Salamanca Pl

Salamanca
Square

**BATTERY
POINT**

Hobart Rivulet

Barrack St

Sandy Bay Rd

Hampden Rd

Molle St

8
Army Museum
of Tasmania

N

0 ——————— 200 m
0 ——————— 0.1 miles

For reviews see

⊙	Sights	p29
✕	Eating	p33
⊖	Drinking	p36
✪	Entertainment	p40
⌂	Shopping	p40

Hobart Real Tennis Club

Sights

Theatre Royal
HISTORIC BUILDING

1 ◉ Map p28, C2

Take a backstage tour of Hobart's prestigious (and very precious) Theatre Royal. Host to bombastic thespians since 1837, and despite a major fire in 1984, it remains Australia's oldest continuously operating theatre. (☏03 6233 2299; www.theatreroyal.com.au; 29 Campbell St; 1hr tour adult/child $15/10; ⊙tours 11am Mon, Wed & Fri)

Hobart Real Tennis Club
HISTORIC BUILDING

2 ◉ Map p28, B4

Dating from 1875, this is one of only three such tennis courts in the southern hemisphere (the others are in Melbourne and Ballarat). Real (or 'Royal') tennis is an archaic form of the highly strung game, played in a jaunty four-walled indoor court. Visitors can watch, take a lesson ($50) or hire the court ($40 per hour per two players). (Royal Tennis Club; ☏03 6231 1781; www.hobarttennis.com.au; 45 Davey St; ⊙9am-6pm Mon-Fri)

Allport Library & Museum of Fine Arts

MUSEUM

3 Map p28, A3

The State Library is home to this excellent collection of rare books on the Australia-Pacific region, as well as colonial paintings, antiques, photographs, manuscripts, decorative arts and furniture. Special exhibits get dusted off for display several times a year, and there are interesting monthly talks and seminars. (☑03 6165 5584; www.linc.tas.gov.au/allport; 91 Murray St; admission free; ⌚9.30am-5pm Mon-Fri, to 2pm Sat)

Gasworks Cellar Door

WINERY

4 Map p28, D2

If you don't have the time (or inclination) to visit Tasmania's wine regions to sip a few cool-climate drops, duck into the Gasworks Cellar Door at the bottom end of Macquarie St instead. Creatively crafted displays take you on a virtual tour, highlighting the best regional bottles (which you can buy here, too). (☑03 6231 5946; www.gasworkscellardoor.com.au; 2 Macquarie St; tastings from $2.50; ⌚noon-4pm Sun-Wed, 11am-5pm Thu-Sat)

Penitentiary Chapel Historic Site

HISTORIC SITE

5 Map p28, B1

The courtrooms, cells and gallows here at 'the Tench' had a hellish reputation in the 1800s: a stint here was to be avoided at all costs. This perhaps goes some way towards explaining how these amazing old convict-built structures have survived in the middle of Hobart in original condition into the 21st century. Take the excellent National Trust–run tour, or the bookings-mandatory **Tench Ghost Tour** (tours $25; ⌚8pm Mon & Fri Jun-Aug, 9pm Mon & Fri Sep-May). (☑03 6231 0911; www.nationaltrust.org.au/places/the-tench; cnr Brisbane & Campbell Sts; tours adult/child/family $15/10/40; ⌚tours 10am, 11.30am, 1pm & 2.30pm Mon-Fri, 1pm & 2.30pm Sat & Sun)

Top Tip

Caught in a One-way Web

Central Hobart's one-way street system can take a while to wrap your head around – is it overly complex for such a compact city? Take the sting out of the experience by leaving the car at your nearby accommodation (astutely booked after reading this) – thus also beating Hobart's dogged parking-meter wardens at their fiendish game.

Markree House Museum MUSEUM

6 Map p28, B5

This backstreet house is a window into life in 1920s Hobart, built for the Baldwin family in 1926 in the 'arts and crafts' architectural style of the day (lots of red brick). The garden is a treat, too. Combined tickets with Narryna Heritage Museum (p101) nearby are great value (adult/child $16/free). (www.tmag.tas.gov.au/markree; 145 Hampden Rd, Battery Point; adult/child $10/4; ⏰10.30am-5pm Sat Oct-Apr, tours 10.30am & 2.30pm Tue-Sun year-round)

St David's Cathedral CHURCH

7 Map p28, C3

Hobart's city-centre cathedral (1823) looks a tad austere, but inside the mood is serene and architecturally uplifting. Duck inside and regain your composure for a minute. Services 8am, 10am and 5.30pm on Sunday. (✆03 6234 4900; www.saintdavids.org.au; 23 Murray St; ⏰8.30am-5pm Mon-Fri, 9am-5pm Sat, 8am-7.30pm Sun)

Army Museum of Tasmania MUSEUM

8 Map p28, B5

The Anglesea Barracks were built adjacent to Battery Point in 1814. Still used by the army, this is the oldest military establishment in Australia. Inside is a volunteer-staffed museum, which runs 45-minute guided tours of the buildings and grounds on Tuesdays. (✆03 6237 7160; www.armymuseumtasmania.org.au; Davey St; adult/child/family $5/1/10; ⏰9am-1pm Tue-Sat, guided tours 11am Tue)

Hobart Comedy Tours CULTURAL

9 Map p28, C3

Laugh it up in Hobart's Franklin Sq with these very punny 'Horrible Hobart' tours (good for families; 11am and 2pm Thursday and Saturday), and more risque 'The (Un) fairer Sex' tours, looking at life as a working girl in old Hobart Town (adults only; 7pm Tuesday and Thursday). Bookings essential. (www.hobartcomedytours.com; tours adult/child from $28/18)

Hobart Historic Tours WALKING

10 Map p28, D3

Informative, entertaining 90-minute walking tours of Hobart and historic Battery Point. There's also an Old Hobart Pub Tour, which sluices through some waterfront watering holes, and a three-hour Grand Hobart Walk. Call or see the website for times and bookings. Reduced winter schedule. (✆03 6234 5550; www.hobarthistorictours.com.au; tours from $30)

Understand

Hobart History

Aboriginal Hobart

Hobart's original inhabitants lived here harmoniously for many thousands of years, maintaining a culture of hunting, fishing and gathering, moving with the seasons and nature's harvest. The semi-nomadic Mouheneenner and Muwinina bands of the Southeast Aboriginal tribe called the area Nibberloonne. Mt Wellington, towering behind Hobart, was a place of refuge for the Muwinina, who called it Kunanyi – a name only recently reassigned to the mountain by the city council.

Colonisation & Convicts

In 1803 the first European arrivals in Van Diemen's Land pitched their tents at Risdon Cove on the Derwent's eastern shore, which became the site of the first massacre of the Mouheneenner. The colony relocated a year later to the site of present-day Hobart, where water running off Mt Wellington was plentiful: today's Hobart Rivulet was the colony's lifeblood.

When Britain's jails overflowed with sinners in the 1820s, tens of thousands of convicts were chained into rotting hulks and shipped down to Hobart Town to serve their sentences in vile conditions. Female convicts were incarcerated at the Female Factory in South Hobart; the worst of the male convicts went to Port Arthur, southeast of the city.

Into the 20th Century

In the 1840s, Hobart's sailors, soldiers, whalers and rapscallions boozed and brawled shamelessly in countless harbourside pubs. It could be argued that the city has only ever partially sobered up – the day Hobart's waterfront is no longer the place to go for a beer will be a sad day indeed – but today's patrons are more likely to be white-collared than bad company at the bar.

With the abolition of convict transportation to Tasmania in 1853, Hobart became marginally more moral and the town came to rely on the apple and wool industries for its fiscal fortitude. In the 20th century Hobart stuttered through the Great Depression and both World Wars, relying on the production of paper, zinc and chocolate, and the deep-water Derwent River harbour to sustain it.

Town Hall

Eating

Bury Me Standing CAFE $

 11 Map p28, B2

Run by a chipper Minnesotan who ended up in Hobart accidentally, this little coffee-and-bagel joint is literally a hole in the wall of a car park. Bagels are pot-boiled (a traditional method ensuring a sticky outer and chewy inner) – don't go past the Reuben version. Couple of milk crates and dinky tables, and Dylan piped through little speakers. Brilliant. (☏0424 365 027; www.facebook.com/burymestandinghobart town; 104 Bathurst St; bagels $5-10; ☺6am-2.30pm Mon-Fri, 7am-2.30pm Sat, coffee only 7am-1pm Sun)

Local Life
Historic Architecture

Locals take for granted the gorgeous crop of heritage stone buildings around central Hobart: take a look at the Theatre Royal (p29), the **Town Hall** (☏03 6238 2765; www.hobartcity. com.au; 50 Macquarie St; admission free; ☺8.15am-5.15pm Mon-Fri), St David's Cathedral (p31) and the marvelously eccentric Hobart Real Tennis Club (p29) for starters.

Farm Gate Market

MARKET $

12 🍴 Map p28, B2

The waterfront Salamanca Market has dominated for decades, but this hyperactive foodie street-mart is giving it a run for its money. Trading commences with the ding of a big brass bell: elbow your way in for the best fruit, veg, honey, wine, baked goods, beer, smoked meats, coffee, cheese, nuts, oils, cut flowers, jams... Terrific! (☎03 6234 5625; www.farmgatemarket.com.au; Bathurst St, btwn Elizabeth & Murray Sts; ⏰8.30am-1pm Sun)

Yellow Bernard

CAFE $

13 🍴 Map p28, B3

With a global selection of interesting blends, Yellow Bernard (great name!) takes its coffee *very* seriously. If you're in a hippie mood, its chai – made with local honey and the cafe's own spice blend – is a perfect way to tune in while wandering Hobart's CBD. Biscuits and corners of cake to go. (☎03 6231 5207; www.yellowbernard.com; 109 Collins St; items from $3; ⏰7am-4pm Mon-Fri)

R Takagi Sushi

JAPANESE $

14 🍴 Map p28, B3

Hobart's best sushi spot – a favourite of Hobart desk jockeys – makes the most of Tasmania's great seafood. Udon noodles and miso also make an appearance. Gorgeous packaging to boot. (☎03 6234 8524; 132 Liverpool St; sushi from $4; ⏰10.30am-5.30pm Mon-Fri, to 4pm Sat, 11.30am-3pm Sun)

Templo

ITALIAN $$

15 🍴 Map p28, A3

Unpretentious little Templo, on a nondescript reach of Patrick St, has assumed the mantle of Hobart's 'must-do' restaurant. With only about 20 seats (bookings essential), and only three or four Italian-inspired mains to choose from, Templo is an exercise in selectivity and sharing (your personal space, and your food). Survey the pricey-but-memorable wine list at the cute bar. (☎03 6234 7659; www.templo.com.au; 98 Patrick St; mains $24-32; ⏰noon-3pm & 6pm-late Thu-Mon)

Understand
Coffee in the City

In this little southern city in a decade not so long ago, caffeine was something that came in instant granules, in a Coke can, or (if you were feeling particularly sophisticated) in a pallid cappuccino at a quasi-Mediterranean takeaway joint. But today, Hobart has truly woken up to real coffee, with a slew of new hole-in-the-wall bean bars opening up in the central city in recent years, and existing cafes lifting their espresso game to keep pace with the city's more discerning coffee palate. Late-night coffee shops have yet to take hold (aspiring Beat writers and Dylan-esque songwriters might have to convene at the pub instead) – but if you've just woken up and need a kick-starter, central Hobart's cafes have got you covered.

Pilgrim Coffee
CAFE $$

16 Map p28, C2

With exposed bricks, timber beams and distressed walls, L-shaped Pilgrim is Hobart's hippest cafe. Expect wraps, panini and interesting mains – Bolivian breakfast bowl! – plus expertly prepared coffee. Fall into conversation with the locals at big shared tables. Down a laneway around the back is the **Standard** (☑03 6234 1999; www.standard-burgers. com; Hudsons La; burgers $7-12; ☺11am-10pm), a burger nook run by the same crew. (☑03 6234 1999; www. pilgrimcoffee.com; 48 Argyle St; mains $15-20; ☺6.30am-4.30pm Mon-Fri, 8am-2pm Sat & Sun)

Small Fry
CAFE $$

17 Map p28, A3

Hip Small Fry sure is small, but what it lacks in size it makes up for in character. Conversation comes

naturally at the shared steel counter: sip some soup, a coffee or a glass of wine; talk, listen, laugh, chew a steak or crunch a salad ... It's a flexible vibe designed to 'avoid labels'. Dig the wooden menu cubes! (☑03 6231 1338; www.small-fryhobart.com.au; 129 Bathurst St; mains $16-26; ☺7.30am-3.30pm Mon-Fri, 8.30am-3.30pm Sat, to 1pm Sun)

Urban Greek
GREEK $$

18 Map p28, A2

Fancy Mediterranean offerings in a former garage, fitted out with bent copper lighting conduits, a timber bar, polished concrete floors and an intimidating Minotaur etched into the copper-plate wall. Expect generous Greek classics done to perfection (moussaka, saganaki, charcoal-grilled octopus), plus imported Greek beers and wines. (☑03 6109 4712; www. facebook.com/urbangreek; 103 Murray St; small plates $12-19; large plates $26-35; ☺5-10pm Tue-Sun)

Understand
The City Vibe

During the day, downtown Hobart is a thriving hive of city workers, shoppers and cafe-goers – the Elizabeth St Mall, Cat & Fiddle Arcade and Centrepoint Arcade are commercially rampant – while multicultural eateries, cafes and little hole-in-the-wall coffee shops keep the office crew fed and fuelled. If you're after some hiking gear, the outdoor shops along Elizabeth St are where it's at. The city centre is also Hobart's public transport hub, with most buses leaving from the lower end of Elizabeth St or adjacent Franklin Sq.

Then, when the sun sets and the workers turn off computers and put on their coats, a kind of social vacuum cleaner sweeps the city streets, sucking up humans and reassigning them to the waterfront. It's true that you won't find a whole lot going on here after dark, but the shops, eateries and Sunday-morning Farm Gate Market are enough to keep you engaged for a few days.

Astor Grill
STEAK $$$

 19 ⊗ Map p28, B4

Indulge in old-school meaty treats at this sumptuous stalwart, in a blood-coloured 1920s brick building on the CBD fringe. Start with some oysters, then choose your prime cut, or perhaps the wallaby fillets with onion mash, beetroot and pepperberry sauce. (☑03 6234 3122; www.astorgrill.com.au; 157 Macquarie St; mains $29-65; ⊗noon-4pm & 5.30-11.45pm Mon-Fri, 5.30-11.45pm Sat)

Franklin
MODERN AUSTRALIAN $$$

20 ⊗ Map p28, C3

In a lofty industrial space (the former *Hobart Mercury* newspaper printing room – the papers would roll straight out the front window), Franklin is all concrete, steel beams, cowhide and curtains. Ignore the cheesy Eric Clapton soundtrack and have a drink at the bar, or settle in for a creative mod Oz meal cooked in the central kitchen. (☑03 6234 3375; www.franklinhobart.com.au; 30 Argyle St; mains $19-41; ⊗8.30am-late Tue-Sat)

Drinking

New Sydney Hotel
PUB

 21 ⊗ Map p28, B2

This low-key city pub is the best boozer in the CBD, with open fires, creative pub food (think duck tongue tortilla; mains $14 to $35) and a terrific 15-tap beer selection, including an ever-changing array of island craft beers (try the Seven Sheds

Hope & Anchor

Local Life

Australia's Oldest Pub?

Depending on who you believe (don't listen to the barman at the Fortune of War in Sydney), the **Hope & Anchor** (☎03 6236 9982; www.hopeandanchor.com.au; 65 Macquarie St; ⏰11.30am-late) in downtown Hobart is the oldest continually licensed pub in Australia (1807). The woody interior is festooned with nautical knick-knacks (duck up the stairs to see the museum-like dining room).

Paradise Pale). Irish jam session 2pm Saturdays, if you're lucky. (☎03 6234 4516; www.newsydneyhotel.com. au; 87 Bathurst St; ⏰noon-10pm Mon, to midnight Tue-Sat, 4-9pm Sun)

Brunswick Hotel PUB

 22 Map p28, B2

Arguably Australia's second-oldest pub (some of the sandstone walls here date back to 1816), the Brunswick has received a schmick makeover dragging it into the current century, with a **backpacker joint** (dm from $29, d without bathroom

Understand
Hotel Horizons

Central Hobart's rather squat, inelegant collation of multistorey buildings looks set to be dwarfed by a new breed of southern skyscrapers, with several major new hotels sitting in the city council's inbox awaiting approval. Singaporean consortium Fragrance Group is behind three new hotel proposals here, including one already being built on Macquarie St, a proposed 120m-high tower on Davey St, and a 75m tower on Collins St. Whoa! Great for the economy and for fixing the city's notorious dearth of beds in the summer season, sure, but opponents are yelling out words like 'overkill', 'glut' and 'what happens in winter?'. Smaller hotel owners, too, are fearing a resultant price-cutting war that will drive them out of business. As always with divisive Tasmanian issues, the situation is a balancing act between vision and preservation, the now and the future, the local and the international. What will Hobart's downtown skyline look like in 10 years?

from $114, d/tr from $155/175; ❄ 🤏)
upstairs and the 'Yard' – an excellent
inner-city beer garden (movies, live
music, trivia, street food etc) – out
the back. (🕿 03 6234 4981; www.
brunswickhotelhobart.com.au; 67 Liverpool
St; ⏰ 11am-late)

Local Life
LGBTI+ Hobart
Hobart's only dedicated gay bar
is **Flamingos Dance Bar** (🕿 03
6294 6173; www.facebook.com/
flamingosdancebar; 201 Liverpool St;
⏰ 10pm-late Fri & Sat) on Liverpool
St in the city centre, with a bedazzling schedule of theme parties
and drag events.

Westend Pumphouse   CAFE, BAR
23 🍷 Map p28, A2

An excellent wine list, good coffee,
and craft beers on tap feature at the
versatile, industrial Pumphouse.
Smash your first coffee of the morning, then come back later in the day
with some friends for shared plates
(mains $19 to $38; try the salt-and-
pepper squid) and a few ales. Live
tunes on Fridays. Kitchen closes
from 2pm to 5pm. (🕿 03 6234 7339;
www.pumphouse.com.au; 105 Murray St;
mains $19-38; ⏰ 8am-late Tue-Sun)

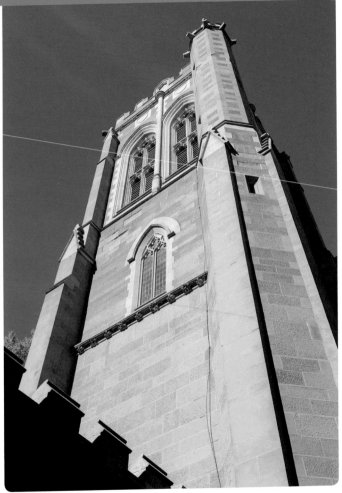

St David's Cathedral (p31)

Entertainment

Playhouse Theatre
THEATRE

24 Map p28, B2

This vintage city theatre is home to the Hobart Repertory Theatre Society (musicals, Shakespeare, kids' plays). Book online. (☏03 6234 1536; www.playhouse.org.au; 106 Bathurst St; ☺box office opens 1hr prior to performances)

Brisbane Hotel
LIVE MUSIC

25 Map p28, B1

The bad old Brisbane has dragged itself up from the pit of old-man, sticky-carpet alcoholism to be reinvented as a progressive, student-filled live-music venue. This is where anyone doing anything original, offbeat or uncommercial gets a gig: punk, metal, hip-hop and singer-songwriters. (☏03 6234 4920; www.facebook.com/

thebrisbanehotelhobart; 3 Brisbane St; ☺5-8.30pm Tue, noon-late Wed-Fri, 4pm-late Sat & Sun)

Grand Poobah
LIVE MUSIC

26 Map p28, B3

This versatile bohemian city bar doubles as a music venue with everything from live bands to DJs, dance, cabaret and comedy. (☏0448 056 163; www.thegrandpoobahbar.com.au; 142 Liverpool St; ☺9pm-late Thu-Sat)

Village Cinemas
CINEMA

27 Map p28, A4

An inner-city multiplex screening mainstream releases. Popcorn galore. (☏1300 555 400; www.villagecinemas.com.au; 181 Collins St; ☺10am-late)

Shopping

Fullers Bookshop
BOOKS

28 Map p28, B3

Hobart's best bookshop has a great range of literature and travel guides, plus regular launches and readings, and the writerly **Afterword Cafe** in the corner. A real hub of the Hobart literary scene for around 70 years. (☏03 6234 3800; www.fullersbookshop.com.au; 131 Collins St; ☺8.30am-6pm Mon-Fri, 9am-5pm Sat, 10am-4pm Sun)

Tasmanian Wine Centre

Tasmanian Wine Centre   WINE

29 🔒 Map p28, A4

Stocks a hefty range of local wines; also organises shipping and tastings for groups. 'The future of Tasmanian wine is sparkling whites', says the boss. (📞03 6234 9995; www. tasmanianwinecentre.com.au; 201 Collins St; ⏱8am-6pm Mon-Fri)

Antiques to Retro   ANTIQUES

30 🔒 Map p28, A3

Interesting furniture, vinyl, books, clothes, glassware and jewellery, old and not-so-old. (📞03 6236 9422; www. antiquestoretro.com.au; 128 Bathurst St; ⏱11am-5pm Mon-Fri, 10am-4pm Sat)

Explore

Salamanca Place & the Waterfront

Ground zero for most Hobart visitors, the waterfront is a broad concrete apron skirting Sullivans Cove, dotted with excellent restaurants, museums and accommodation. The vibe is bright, breezy and buzzy. Nearby is Salamanca Place, a well-preserved row of old sandstone warehouses hosting galleries, cafes, restaurants, pubs and bars. Salamanca Market erupts here every Saturday morning.

The Sights in a Day

☀ Salamanca's breakfast spots are myriad, but the coffee at **Retro Cafe** (p59) never disappoints. This is a real day-turns-to-night precinct – there's always something going on. But for now, bee-line towards **Mawson's Huts Replica Museum** (p56) by Constitution Dock – an authentic insight into Antarctic life. Not enough nautical? The **Maritime Museum of Tasmania** (p56) is just up Argyle St.

☀ A takeaway fish-and-chip lunch from **Flippers** (p59) on Constitution Dock is hard to beat. Marginally more formal is **Fish Frenzy** (p59). Afterwards, stroll around Victoria Dock and cast an eye over Hobart's fishing fleet. Back on Salamanca, the shops and galleries inside the **Salamanca Arts Centre** (p56) proffer the best of local arts and crafts. Duck into **Tricycle Cafe & Bar** (p60) for an afternoon coffee shot.

☽ For a pre-dinner drink, try **Jack Greene** (p63), then take your pick of Salamanca's brilliant restaurants: **Maldini** (p60) is an enduring favourite. Later on, glam-up your evening with cocktails and water views at **Glass House** (p63) inside Brooke St Pier.

For a local's day on the waterfront, see p52.

 Top Sights

Salamanca Place (p44)

Tasmanian Museum & Art Gallery (p48)

Local Life

On The Waterfront (p52)

♥ Best of Hobart

Eating
Retro Cafe (p59)
Flippers (p59)
Fish Frenzy (p59)
Blue Eye (p61)
Aloft (p60)
Frank (p61)

Drinking
Hobart Brewing Company (p63)
Jack Green (p63)
Glass House (p63)
T-42° (p63)
Grape (p65)

Getting There

✈ **Walk** Parking here is a drag; ditch the wheels and walk.

🚍 **Bus** Bus services into Salamanca Place and the waterfront areas are affordable.

🚕 **Taxi** Cab-it in from North Hobart or Sandy Bay.

Top Sights
Salamanca Place

Dating back to Hobart's whaling and sailing heyday of the 1830s, Salamanca Place is a photogenic, 500m-long row of three- and four-storey sandstone warehouses. Gone are the sailors, whalers and wares: the buildings now host a fantastic collection of restaurants, cafes, bars, galleries, shops, pubs and performance spaces. The famed Salamanca Market consumes the entire street every Saturday morning.

www.salamanca.com.au

Eating & Drinking

Interesting fact for the day: Salamanca Place takes its name from the Spanish province of Salamanca, where the Duke of Wellington claimed victory in the Battle of Salamanca in 1812. Something to discuss over a meal or an evening drink, perhaps – eating and drinking being the prime reasons you're here! So popular is the Salamanca scene that the Hobart City Council recently widened the footpath in front of the warehouses, to allow restaurants and bars more space for street-side tables and chairs. Wander along and see what kindles your appetite.

Salamanca Market

What started out as a couple of hippies selling raspberries in 1972 has evolved into a kilometre-long frenzy of food and commerce that consumes all of Salamanca Place every Saturday morning. With thousands of people here every week, Salamanca Market (p66) is something to behold: give yourself at least a few hours to wander its length and back again, a slow-shuffling circuit down one side of the stalls then back down the other. The cafes overflow, the buskers are in fine voice and (even when it's cold and wet) the atmosphere is downright convivial.

Salamanca Square

The big flat space out the back of Salamanca Place was once a quarry and then a car park. Then, in the mid-1990s, Salamanca Sq emerged. An adjunct, traffic-free space to the main thoroughfare, it's host to some great cafes and bars; the Hobart Book Shop (p69), one of the city's best; and Kathmandu (p69), the runaway-success outdoor company founded by resident

☑ Top Tips

▶ Parking here can be a drag, even in the quietest of seasons (don't even think about it during the Saturday morning Salamanca Market); walk instead.

▶ For the pick of the fresh produce and antique knick-knacks, arrive at Salamanca Market early (8am should do it).

▶ Plan on spending at least a full day here: you'll need that long to digest your breakfast, lunch, afternoon tea, dinner…

✕ Take a Break

The list of Salamanca Place eating options might be long, but keep Retro Cafe (p59) at the top for coffee or brunch.

Jack Greene (p63) is open from lunchtime till late for beery libations.

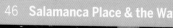

Handmark Gallery at the Salamanca Arts Centre (p67)

Understand
Shifting Shoreline

It's hard to imagine now, but the Salamanca Place warehouses were once a lot closer to the water than they are today. No, the warehouses haven't moved, but the shoreline has: the broad concrete apron now skirting the whole of Sullivans Cove is largely built over reclaimed land. Merchants were once able to sail their ships right up to the front of the warehouses to offload/load their goods with ease (imagine how annoyed they'd be today!).

Tasmanian Jan Cameron. There's also a kid-magnet fountain here and a few sunny patches of lawn to loll around on.

Salamanca Arts Centre

As with many of Tasmania's architectural relics, the Salamanca Place warehouses only survived the 20th century because no-one here had the money to knock them down. Thank goodness! Indeed, these chunky stone walls would take some shifting: step into the Salamanca Arts Centre (p56) for a close-up look...oh, and to check out the dozens of artists' studios, retail spaces, performance venues,

Salamanca Market (p66)

GRANT DIXON / GETTY IMAGES ©

TRAVELGAME / GETTY IMAGES ©

Understand
RIP Knopwoods

For many decades, every Hobartian's favourite boozer was Knopwoods Retreat, a snug pub on Salamanca Place. Every Friday night the city's post-work crowd convened and spilled across the street. These were less OH&S–obsessed days, with winter oil-drum fires, traffic nudging through the crowd and minstrels playing on the concrete awning above the door. But time and tastes change: the drinkers were drawn to hipper venues and 'Knoppies' closed in 2015. The Whaler (p64) pub is here now – a decent spot for a beer, but with big memories to compete with.

cafes and galleries that comprise this artsy co-op.

Running since 1975, the SAC has become a vital hub of Hobart's artistic life, maintaining a hectic program of launches, events and performances to bolster its heady retail trade. If you're here on a Friday night, don't miss 'Rektango' at the **Salamanca Arts Centre Courtyard** (www.salarts.org.au/rektango; 77 Salamanca Pl; ⊙5.30-7.30pm Fri) – a free evening performance by one of several regular folk/world-music bands.

Locals roll in, have a drink, a dance and generally let their hair down.

Hungry? Grab a coffee or some lunch at Tricycle Cafe & Bar (p60) or a bang-up Greek meal at Mezethes (p60), both tenants in the SAC complex.

Top Sights
Tasmanian Museum & Art Gallery

Incorporating Hobart's oldest building, the Commissariat Store (1808), this revamped museum features Aboriginal and colonial art and relics, and excellent history and wildlife displays.

'TMAG', as it's known to friends and associates, occupies a special place in Hobartians' minds and memories. Every school kid in the city has seen these rooms and walked these halls at some stage, returning again as adults to experience the best collections of Tasmanian art and artefacts in the state.

TMAG

☏ 03 6165 7000

www.tmag.tas.gov.au

Dunn Pl

admission free

🕑 10am-4pm daily Jan-Mar, 10am-4pm Tue-Sun Apr-Dec

Custom House, part of the TMAG precinct

Museum Highlights

Some of the most interesting things to see at the museum actually are the museum – historic buildings that form part of this huge, whole-city-block complex include the **Bond Store** (1824), **Commissariat Complex** (1808 – Tasmania's oldest surviving public building) and the **Private Secretary's Cottage** (1813), a little colonial cottage completely encircled by the museum.

Inside, don't miss the **Thylacine Gallery** on Level 1, telling the sad tale of the now (probably) extinct Tasmanian Tiger; and the **ningina tunapri** Tasmanian Aboriginal gallery, also on Level 1, which shines a light on Tasmania's oldest culture and country.

Nature-lovers will get a kick out of the **Tasmania: Earth & Life** display on Level 1, which digs into the island's geology and kooky contingent of flora and fauna.

Tasmanian Art

The main art galleries here are on the top floor (Level 2), with three spaces exhibiting a permanent collection of colonial, mid- and late-20th-century art, plus decorative arts. The colonial collection is particularly engaging, entitled 'Dispossessions and Possessions', with treasured works by arty notables such as Benjamin Duterreau and John Glover. The 20th-century galleries take a look at the influence of modernism on Tasmanian art, and the funky arts-and-crafts revival that happened here in the 1960s and '70s.

Guided Tours

Running from Wednesday to Sunday, free guided tours explore different areas of this sprawling, multilevel complex. Tours depart the main entry at 1pm and 2pm from September

☑ Top Tips

▶ Download a visitor map and guide from www.tmag.tas.gov.au (click on 'What's On' then 'Plan Your Visit').

▶ Free guided tours are a TMAG introduction. No bookings – just turn up (tours at 1pm and 2pm from Wednesday to Sunday).

▶ The Museum Shop sells Hobart's best travel-sized gifts (skip the tourist-tat in the Elizabeth St Mall).

✕ Take a Break

The museum's **Courtyard Cafe** (☎03 6165 7002; www.facebook.com/museumcourtyardcafe; Tasmanian Museum & Art Gallery, Dunn Pl; mains $6-16; ⏱9am-4pm Mon-Fri, 10am-4pm Sat & Sun Jan-Mar, 9am-4pm Tue-Fri, 10am-4pm Sat & Sun Apr-Dec) is good for coffee and cake.

Across Macquarie St from the museum is Australia's oldest pub, the Hope & Anchor (p37).

Understand
Hadley's Gallery

A new installation sponsored by TMAG is the Hadley's Gallery at **Hadley's Orient Hotel** (☏ 03 6237 2999; www.hadleyshotel.com. au; 34 Murray St; d/f from $160/245, 2-bedroom apt from $370; P ❄ @ ☏) on Murray St in central Hobart. Inside is a fascinating display of 29 historic prints, capturing long-lost views of colonial Hobart and the Derwent River – a precious cache of images offering a detailed insight into life on the river and in old Hobart Town.

to May, and at 1.30pm from June to August. The 1pm tour visits the Welcome Garden and historic Commissariat Complex and Bond Store; the 2pm tour takes you into the main permanent exhibition and gallery spaces on Levels 1 and 2. The 1.30pm tour adopts a 'Winter Highlights' theme, relating some quirky TMAG tales.

Also on offer are free themed and exhibition-specific tours running at 11am daily, Wednesday to Sunday. It's a changing program – check with the visitor information desk to see what's scheduled.

GRANT DIXON / GETTY IMAGES ©

Kids' Stuff

Fully committed to showing your kids a good time, the museum runs dedicated family days on the last Sunday of every month, with heaps of hands-on, creative, interpretive experiences cued-up to help the little tackers get a handle on history. Similarly rich and educative are TMAG's excellent school holiday programs: download a schedule of what's happening from www.tmag.tas.gov.au/learning_and_discovery/families.

On any day, free Discovery Backpacks (ages seven to 12) and Museum Toolkits (ages four to seven) are available from the front desk, filled with interesting objects and activities to help kids experience different aspects of the museum: history, art, the Southern Ocean, Antarctica and natural science.

Local Life
On the Waterfront

Hobart and the Derwent River are inextricably linked: the river sustained Aboriginal Tasmanians for millenniums; the river brought the English here in 1803; the river was Hobart's link to the world as it grew from a far-flung convict outpost. Take a walk around the waterfront to catch the nautical vibes.

❶ Parliamentary Proceedings
From Salamanca Place, track across the lawns to ogle **Parliament House** (☏ 03 6212 2200; www.parliament.tas.gov.au/parliament/tours.htm; Parliament Sq; admission free; ☺ tours 10am & 2pm Mon-Fri on nonsitting days), originally built in 1840 as Hobart's customs house, keeping tabs on goods coming in and out of the port.

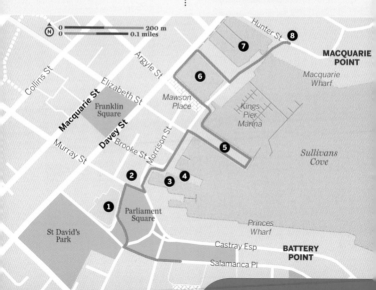

❷ Thirsty Work

Just across Murray St, the three-tiered, sandstone **Customs House Hotel** (📞03 6234 6645; www.customshousehotel.com; 1 Murray St; ⏱7am-late Mon-Fri, 8am-late Sat & Sun), which was licensed in 1846, is linked to Parliament House via a secret tunnel under the road (thirsty work, legislation). It's a gritty, no-frills harbourside boozer – one of the last pubs on the waterfront to have resisted hipster-era trappings.

❸ Watermans Dock

Head for the water across Morrison St: Watermans Dock is the most modest of Hobart's docks, named for the watermen who ferried people around Hobart's shores in the mid-1800s. If the tide is low, traverse the concrete steps at the head of the dock.

❹ Brooke St Pier

The flashy new floating Brooke St Pier is where you catch the ferry to **MONA** (Museum of Old & New Art; 📞03 6277 9900; www.mona.net.au; 655 Main Rd, Berriedale; adult/child $25/free, Tasmanian residents free; ⏱10am-6pm daily Jan, 10am-6pm Wed-Mon Feb-Apr & Dec, 10am-5pm Wed-Mon May-Nov). It's a far cry from the old wooden ferry pier that became extremely busy when Hobart's Tasman Bridge collapsed in 1975, and commuter ferries criss-crossed the river.

❺ Elizabeth St Pier

Most of the elegantly proportioned Elizabeth St Pier is consumed by an apartment hotel, eateries and bars.

Walk out to the end and peer into the depths – Sullivans Cove is the world's second-deepest natural harbour (after Sydney).

❻ Constitution Dock

When the bedraggled boats in the **Sydney to Hobart Yacht Race** (p59) sail into town every New Year's Eve, Constitution Dock turns into party central. The rest of the year it's a rather soupy square of sea, with a line of takeaway fish punts along its northern shore.

❼ Victoria Dock

If Constitution Dock is a party place, Victoria Dock is all about hard work. This is where Hobart's fleet of deep-sea fishing trawlers moors: count crayfish pots as you cross the swing bridge to Hunter St.

❽ Hunter St Warehouses

Facing off with the Salamanca Place warehouses across Sullivans Cove, the Hunter St warehouses are more eclectic, hosting restaurants, bars, the University of Tasmania School of Art and the outstanding **Henry Jones Art Hotel** (📞03 6210 7700; www.thehenryjones.com; 25 Hunter St; d from $340; 🅿❄@🛜). Hunter St was once a sandy isthmus extending to little Hunter Island, long-since buried beneath the wharves. Grab a glassful at the **IXL Long Bar** (⏱5-10.30pm Mon-Thu, 3-10.30pm Fri & Sat, 5-9pm Sun) inside the Henry Jones.

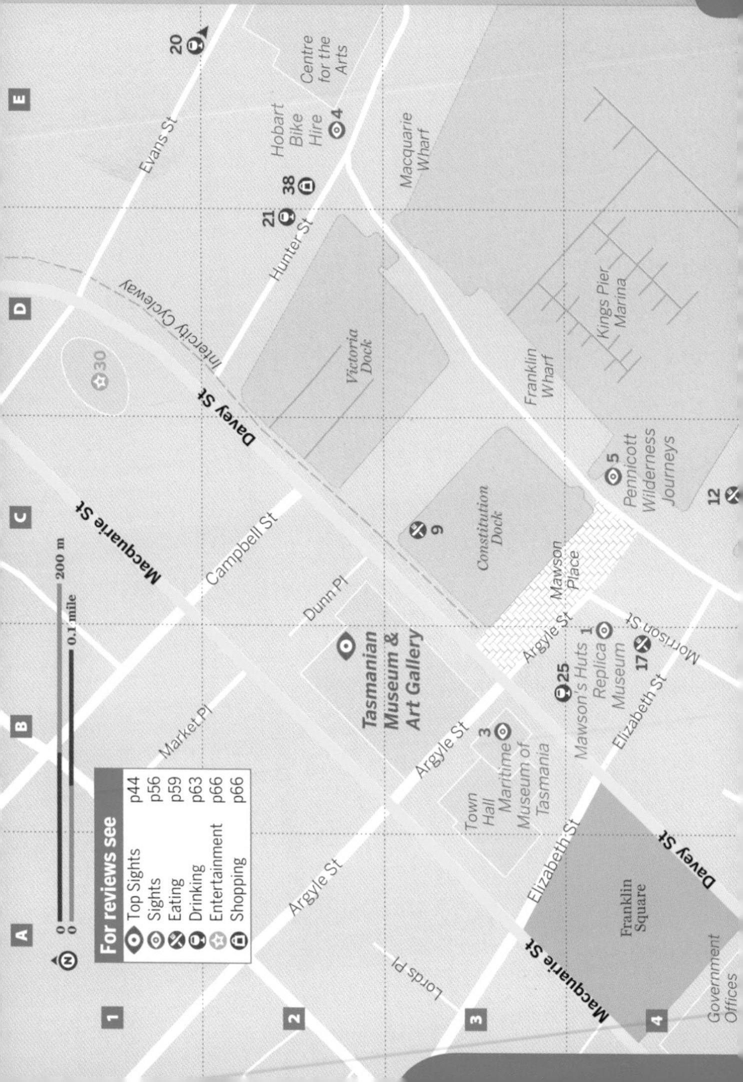

20 ►H

Centre
for the
Arts

Hobart
Bike
Hire   ◉ 4

38 ⓘ⊞

21 ⓘ
Hunter St

Macquarie
Wharf

Kings Pier
Marina

Intercity Cycleway

✿ 30

Davey St

Franklin
Wharf

Campbell St

Victoria
Dock

◉ 5
Pennicott
Wilderness
Journeys

Macquarie St

⊗ 9

Constitution
Dock

12 ⊗

Dunn Pl

Mawson
Place

**Tasmanian
Museum &
Art Gallery**   ◉

Argyle St

Mawson's Huts 1
Replica
Museum

⊗ 17

Morrison St

Market Pl

Argyle St

Maritime 3
Museum of
Tasmania   ◉

Town
Hall

ⓘ 25

Elizabeth St

Davey St

Argyle St

Elizabeth St

Franklin
Square

Lords Pl

Macquarie St

Government
Offices

200 m
0.1 mile

Sullivans Cove

Elizabeth St Pier

Princes Wharf

Red Decker

Brooke St Pier

23 Pier

Castray Esp

Morrison St

Tasmanian Whisky Tours

Hobart Historic Cruises

22

16 7 6

8

11

Murray St

Despard St

Brooke St

Parliament Square

Parliament House

Commonwealth Law Courts

St David's Park

Gladstone St

Salamanca Place

33

13 19 28

27 37 35

26

24 10

36

31

Salamanca Arts Centre

Salamanca Pl

Kelly's Steps

Woobys La

Salamanca Square

BATTERY POINT

Montpellier Rt

32

34 2 14 29 15

18

Runnymede St

Princes Park

McGregor St

Battery Sq

Sights

Mawson's Huts Replica Museum
MUSEUM

1 Map p54, B4

This excellent waterfront installation is an exact model of one of the huts in which Sir Douglas Mawson hunkered down on his 1911–14 Australasian Antarctic Expedition, which set sail from Hobart. Inside it is 100% authentic, right down to the matches, the stove and the bunks. A knowledgable guide sits at a rustic table, ready to answer your Antarctic enquiries. Entry fees go towards the upkeep of the original huts at Cape Denison in Antarctica. (📞03 6231 1518, 1300 551 422; www.mawsons-huts-replica.org.au; cnr Morrison & Argyle Sts; adult/child/family $12/4/28; ⊙9am-6pm Oct-Apr, 10am-5pm May-Sep)

Salamanca Arts Centre
ARTS CENTRE

2 Map p54, C7

The non-profit Salamanca Arts Centre has been here since the '70s and occupies seven Salamanca warehouses. It's home to dozens of arts organisations and individuals, including excellent shops, galleries, studios, performing-arts venues, a couple of cafes, and public spaces. Don't miss the free Friday evening 'Rektango' folk/world-music gigs in the Salamanca Arts Centre Courtyard (p47) out the back. (SAC; 📞03 6234 8414; www.salarts.org.au; 77 Salamanca Pl; ⊙shops & galleries 9am-5pm)

Maritime Museum of Tasmania
MUSEUM

3 Map p54, B3

Highlighting shipwrecks, boat building, whaling and Hobart's unbreakable bond with the sea, the Maritime Museum of Tasmania (out the back of the Town Hall) has an interesting (if a little static) collection of photos, paintings, models and relics (try to resist ringing the huge brass bell from the *Rhexenor*). (📞03 6234 1427; www.maritimetas.org; 16 Argyle St; adult/child/family $10/8/20; ⊙9am-5pm)

Hobart Bike Hire
CYCLING

4 Map p54, E2

Located just in from the Brooke Street Pier, this bike hire shop has lots of ideas for self-guided tours around the city or along the Derwent River to MONA. Maps and helmets included; kids' trailers and tandems are also available. (📞0447 556 189; www.hobartbikehire.com.au; 1A Brooke Street; bike hire per day/overnight from $25/35; ⊙9am-5pm)

Pennicott Wilderness Journeys
BOATING

5 Map p54, C4

Pennicott offers half-a-dozen outstanding boat trips around key southern Tasmanian sights, including trips to Bruny Island, Tasman Island, the

Maritime Museum of Tasmania

Tasman Peninsula, D'Entrecasteaux Channel and the Iron Pot Lighthouse south of Hobart. The **Tasmanian Seafood Seduction** (www.seafoodseduction.com.au) trip is a winner for fans of all things fishy. (☏ 03 6234 4270; www.pennicottjourneys.com.au; Dock Head Bldg, Franklin Wharf; tours adult/child from $225/155; ⊙ 7am-6.30pm)

Gourmania WALKING

Fabulous, flavour-filled walking tours around Salamanca Place and central Hobart, with plenty of opportunities to try local foods and chat to restaurant, cafe and shop owners. (☏ 0419 180 113; www.gourmaniafoodtours.com.au; tours from $89)

Tasmanian Whisky Tours DISTILLERY

6 ◉ Map p54, B5

Tasmanian whisky has been getting plenty of press since Sullivans Cove Whisky won the coveted 'Best Single Malt' gong at the World Whisky Awards in 2014. Take a day tour with this passionate outfit, visiting three distilleries with tastings of top Tassie single malts. Minimum four passengers. Beer and wine tours also available. (☏ 0412 099 933; www.tasmanianwhiskytours.com.au; tours $249; ⊙ Tue, Fri & Sat)

Understand
Macquarie Point & MONA

What an opportunity! The vast area of industrial port land known as Macquarie Point, adjacent to Hobart's waterfront, is ripe for redevelopment. In 2016, the founder of MONA, eccentric/genius David Walsh, announced plans to build a $2 billion cultural precinct here, acknowledging and celebrating 40,000 years of continuous Aboriginal history in the state. Visionary and long overdue in its intent towards reconciliation, certainly, but opponents claim ongoing port functions, including logging exports, are at odds with tourism and that the two could not co-exist. Hobart's Lord Mayor also weighed in, suggesting that such a project might be 'guilt-ridden' if not done tastefully (…perhaps she'd seen the infamous poop machine at MONA). Whatever happens, if David Walsh is involved, it's sure to be interesting – watch this space!

Red Decker
BUS

7 Map p54, C5

Commentated sightseeing on an old London double-decker bus. Buy a 20-stop, hop-on-hop-off pass (valid for one or two days), or do the tour as a 90-minute loop. Pay a bit more and add a Cascade Brewery tour (adult/child $65/55) or Mt Wellington tour ($65/40) to the deal. (☑03 6236 9116; www.reddecker.com.au; 20-stop pass adult/child/family 24hr $35/20/90, 48hr $40/25/100)

Hobart Historic Cruises
CRUISE

8 Map p54, B6

Chug up or down the Derwent River from Hobart's waterfront on cute old ferries. Also runs longer lunch (adult/child/family $35/35/120) and dinner ($58/55/180) cruises travelling both up and down the river. Call for times and bookings. (☑03 6200 9074; www.hobarthistoriccruises.com.au; Murray St Pier; 1hr cruises adult/child/family $25/22.50/70)

Tours Tasmania
TOURS

Small-group full-day trips from Hobart, including trips to Port Arthur, Hastings Caves and a 'Mt Field, Wildlife & Mt Wellington' tour with lots of walks and waterfalls (adult/concession $130/120). Park fees included; BYO lunch. (☑1800 777 103; www.tourstas.com.au)

Eating

Flippers

FISH & CHIPS $

9 Map p54, C3

There are quite a few floating fish punts moored in Constitution Dock, selling fresh-caught seafood either uncooked or cooked. Our pick is Flippers, an enduring favourite with a voluptuous fish-shaped profile. Fillets of flathead and curls of calamari – straight from the deep blue sea and into the deep fryer. The local seagulls will adore you. (☑03 6234 3101; www.flippersfishandchips. com.au; Constitution Dock; meals $10-28; ⏰9.30am-8.30pm)

Retro Cafe

CAFE $

10 Map p54, B7

So popular it hurts, funky Retro is ground zero for Saturday brunch among the market stalls (or any day, really). Masterful breakfasts, bagels, salads and burgers interweave with laughing staff, chilled-out jazz and the whirr and bang of the coffee machine. A classic Hobart cafe. (☑03 6223 3073; 31 Salamanca Pl; mains $11-17; ⏰7.30am-6pm Mon-Fri, 8am-4pm Sat & Sun)

Daci & Daci

BAKERY, CAFE $

11 Map p54, A5

Full of public servants and parliamentarians on the loose, Daci & Daci is an excellent bakery-cafe serving quiches, pasties, salads, sandwiches, pies (try the lamb, red wine and rosemary version) and cloud-like meringues the size of softballs. Sit inside if it's wet, or on the split-level street-side deck if it's not. (☑03 6224 9237; www.dacianddacibakers. com.au; 11 Murray St; mains $8-20; ⏰7am-6pm)

Fish Frenzy

SEAFOOD $$

12 Map p54, C4

A casual, waterside fish nook, overflowing with fish fiends and brimming with fish and chips, fishy salads (warm octopus with yoghurt dressing) and fish burgers. The

 Local Life

Sydney to Hobart Yacht Race

Arguably the world's greatest and most treacherous open-ocean yacht race, the Sydney to Hobart Yacht Race (www.rolexsydneyhobart. com; ⏰Dec) winds up at Hobart's Constitution Dock some time around New Year's Eve. As the storm-battered maxis limp across the finish line, champagne corks pop and weary sailors turn the town upside down. On New Year's Day, find a sunny spot by the harbour, munch some lunch from the **Taste of Tasmania** (p144) food festival and count spinnakers on the river. New Year's resolutions? What New Year's resolutions?

eponymous 'Fish Frenzy' ($21) delivers a little bit of everything. Quality can be inconsistent, but good staff and buzzy harbourside vibes compensate. No bookings. (📞03 6231 2134; www.fishfrenzy.com.au; Elizabeth St Pier; mains $15-35; ⏱11am-9pm; 🖥🚸)

Maldini
ITALIAN $$

13 Map p54, B7

A midrange Italian joint steadily climbing the culinary rungs, with essential pasta and risotto dishes offered alongside peppy mains such as Sicilian fish stew, osso bucco and baked calamari. Tiramisu and grappa polish the palate and close out the night. Lovely interiors. (📞03 6223 4460; www.maldinirestaurant. com.au; 47 Salamanca Pl; mains $27-32; ⏱8am-late)

Local Life
University of Tasmania School of Art

One of the first redevelopments of the Hunter St warehouses on Sullivans Cove's northern shore involved the University of Tasmania School of Art moving into the old IXL jam factory in the 1980s. The students are still here, looking unwashed and somewhat slightly dazed as multi-million-dollar wharf redevelopments and apartment complexes pop up all around them.

Tricycle Cafe & Bar
CAFE $$

14 Map p54, C8

This cosy red-painted nook inside the Salamanca Arts Centre (p56) serves up a range of cafe classics (BLTs, toasties, scrambled free-range eggs, salads, house-brewed chai and Fair Trade coffee), plus awesome daily specials (braised Wagyu rice bowl with jalapeño cream – wow!). Wines by the glass from the bar. (📞03 6223 7228; 77 Salamanca Pl; mains $12-20; ⏱8.30am-4pm Mon-Sat)

Mezethes
GREEK $$

15 Map p54, C8

Tried and true Greek dishes and Adonis-like staff come together perfectly at Mezethes. All the classics (moussaka, souvlaki, lamb, fish, saganaki, baklava) plus, in true Hellenic style, a dazzling array of starters. The entrée platter ($32 for two) is hard to beat. Grab an outdoor table on a warm evening. (📞03 6224 4601; www.mezethes.com. au; off Woobys La, 77 Salamanca Pl; mains breakfast $12-17, lunch & dinner $15-32; ⏱8.30am-late)

Aloft
MODERN AUSTRALIAN $$$

16 Map p54, C5

Staking a bold claim as Hobart's top restaurant, Aloft occupies a lofty eyrie in the floating Brooke Street Pier. Menu hits include the likes of yellow fish curry with beetroot and fennel, and steamed oysters with

Daci & Daci (p59)

fermented chilli. If you can drag your gaze away from the view, service and presentation are both excellent, in an unpretentious Hobart kinda way. (☑03 6223 1619; www.aloftrestaurant. com; Brooke St Pier; mains $34-35, Fri set lunch $30, banquets from $70; ⊙6pm-late Tue-Sat)

Frank SOUTH AMERICAN $$$

17 Map p54, B4

At the base of the much-maligned Marine Board Building, Frank brings fabulous South American–inspired flavours to the Hobart waterfront. Everything is designed for sharing, from empanadas to small plates (crispy squid,

confit lamb ribs), vegetable dishes (charred sweet potato and goats' curd), and sensational steaks. Frank is one well dressed hombre, with super-hip interior design. (☑03 6231 5005; www.frankrestaurant.com.au; 1 Franklin Wharf; mains $31-47; ⊙11am-10.30pm Mon-Sat)

Blue Eye SEAFOOD $$$

18 Map p54, D7

Ignore the slightly clinical decor and dive into some of Hobart's best seafood. Stand-outs include scallop and prawn linguine, curried seafood chowder, and a terrific seafood pie with parsley-and-spinach cream. Moo Brew pilsner on tap

Understand

Hobart's Antarctic Links

Tasmania was the last chunk of Gondwanaland to break free from Antarctica, which is now about 2500km south of Hobart. As the planet heats up and scientists forecast melting Antarctic ice, Hobart is becoming one of the world's leading Antarctic research and gateway cities.

Antarctic Research

The Australian Antarctic Division has its HQ in suburban Kingston, south of Hobart, but there's also the CSIRO Marine and Atmospheric Research facility, in Battery Point. And just across the road from Salamanca Place is the University of Tasmania's sleek Institute of Antarctic and Southern Ocean Studies building (also home to the Antarctic Climate and Ecosystems Cooperative Research Centre, tasked with understanding Antarctica's role in the global climate system and projecting climate change impacts).

The Antarctic Division's garish orange research vessel *Aurora Australis* and the CSIRO's *Investigator* (and, in the past, the *Southern Surveyor* and *Franklin*) are regulars at the Hobart wharves. The *Aurora Australis*, in particular, has become a Hobart icon, much photographed and welcomed into port like a returning warrior.

Mawson's Huts

Next to Constitution Dock on the Hobart waterfront, the fascinating Mawson's Huts Replica Museum (p56) recreates the famed explorer Douglas Mawson's century-old Antarctic huts in intricate detail.

To much fanfare, Mawson and his crew of 18 set sail from Hobart in 1911, bound for the great southern continent, still largely unknown at the time (no-one had set foot on Antarctica prior to 1895). When Mawson arrived, he and his men built four timber huts at Cape Denison and established the first permanent Australian Antarctic base.

Mawson's huts are still standing, but, under constant assault by the weather, are in various states of disrepair: all profits from this museum go towards their preservation. Inside, the museum is brilliantly detailed and atmospheric: it's not hard to imagine 19 men living and working in these cramped confines, while outside the blizzards raged.

and a Tasmanian-skewed wine list complete a very zesty picture. (☎03 6223 5297; www.blueeye.net.au; 1 Castray Esplanade; mains $25-40; ☺5-9pm Mon, 11am-9pm Tue-Sat)

Drinking

Jack Greene
BAR

19 🍷 Map p54, C7

The gourmet burgers here nudge $20, but atmospheric Jack Greene (a European hunting lodge on the run?) is worthwhile if you're a wandering beer fan. Glowing racks of bottled brews fill the fridges, and there are at least 16 beers on tap from around Australia and New Zealand. Occasional acoustic troubadours perch next to the stairs. (☎03 6224 9655; www.jackgreene.com.au; 49 Salamanca Pl; ☺11.30am-late)

Hobart Brewing Company
CRAFT BEER

20 🍷 Map p54, E1

In a big shed on Macquarie Point, fronted by the Red Square community space, Hobart Brewing Company has been doing good things with beer. There are plenty of creative brews on tap (try the St Christopher cream ale, or a $10 tasting paddle), plus there's live music most weekends and often-laughing staff. (☎03 6231 9779; www.hobartbrewingco.com. au; 16 Evans St; ☺4-10pm Thu, to 11pm Fri, 2-11pm Sat, 11am-6pm Sun)

IXL Long Bar
BAR

21 🍷 Map p54, D2

Prop yourself at the glowing bar at the Henry Jones Art Hotel (p53) and check out Hobart's fashionistas over a honey porter. If there are no spare stools at the bar, flop onto the leather couches in the hotel lobby. Moo Brew on tap, killer whiskies and live jazz Friday and Saturday. (☎03 6210 7700; www.thehenryjones. com; Henry Jones Art Hotel, 25 Hunter St; ☺5-10.30pm Mon-Thu, 3-10.30pm Fri & Sat, 5-9pm Sun)

T-42°
BAR

22 🍷 Map p54, C5

Stylish waterfront T-42° makes a big splash with its food (mains $19 to $35), but also draws well-dressed, late-week barflies with its minimalist interior, spinnaker-shaped bar and ambient tunes. If you stay out late enough, breakfast offers redemption from any nocturnal misdemeanours. (☎03 6224 7742; www.tav42.com.au; Elizabeth St Pier; ☺7.30am-late)

Glass House
COCKTAIL BAR

23 🍷 Map p54, C5

The very fancy Glass House sits in the prow of the floating Brooke Street Pier, a huge window-wall affording uninterrupted views down the Derwent River estuary. Put on your best duds, order a Hobartian Sidecar and soak it all in. Fab bar food, too (small plates $18 to $30). Is Charlie, the quintessential Hobart barman, working tonight? (☎0437 245 540; www.theglass.house; Brooke St Pier; ☺noon-10pm Mon & Tue, to midnight Wed-Sun)

Waterman's Beer Market
CRAFT BEER

24 Map p54, B7

'Since 1840' is the tag-line here…well, the building maybe. But 'WBM' is one of a new brigade of Salamanca Place booze rooms, focused on excellent craft and small-batch beers and regular live music. Order a pint of Harbour Master Ale from Hobart Brewing Company (p63) and head for the moody row of booths. Cheap jugs Wednesday night. (☎0477 814 782; www.watermansbeermarket.com.au; 27 Salamanca Pl; ☺11am-late)

Lark Distillery
DISTILLERY

25 Map p54, B3

Lark Distillery was a trailblazer in Tasmania's surge into the world of single malt whisky. Stop by for a drink, a tasting session ($20), or a two-hour tour of the distillery ($75), a 20-minute drive from the cellar door. Order a cheese board, work your way along the whisky wall, or sip a Moo Brew if you'd prefer. (☎03 6231 9088; www.larkdistillery.com; 14 Davey St; ☺10.30am-7pm Thu-Sun, 10.30am-late Fri & Sat)

Whaler
PUB

26 Map p54, B7

Until the end of 2015 this pub was called 'Knopwoods Retreat', an endearing old boozer and a perennial Friday-night favourite. The Whaler is doing its best to live up to the tradition, its unpretentious service and interiors making it something

---

Understand
Life by the Harbour

These waterside precincts embody Hobart at its most hyperactive. Well, maybe just active. Either way, the visual appeal of the Salamanca Place sandstone warehouses and shimmering Sullivans Cove with its waterfront bars, pubs, restaurants and resident fishing fleet is undeniable (bring your camera). There are enough places to eat and drink here to keep you busy for months, but give yourself a few days to soak it all up – perhaps starting at the Salamanca Place side of the cove, working your way around the waterfront and back again. Even if you leave the area to shop, check out museums, visit MONA etc, you'll probably find yourself drawn back here at night when the pubs and bars really get rockin'.

GRANT DIXON / GETTY IMAGES ©

Lark Distillery

of an incongruity on the otherwise highly polished Salamanca Place. (📞03 6200 1854; www.facebook.com/thewhalersreturn; 39 Salamanca Pl; 🕐11am-late)

Barcelona
BAR

27 🚇 Map p54, B8

Lots of different beers on tap, a slick wine list and well-priced bistro-style food (mains $20 to $30) make this one of Salamanca's most versatile drinking spots. The outdoor tables are perfect for suit-watching during the day, while cheap pints lure the students on Wednesday nights. DJs Wednesday, Friday and Saturday. (📞03 6224 7557; www.barcelonahobart. com; 23 Salamanca Sq; 🕐noon-late Mon-Fri, 9am-late Sat & Sun)

Grape
WINE BAR

28 🚇 Map p54, C7

In search of civility amid the nocturnal Salamanca fray? Grape is possibly your best bet, a woody wine bar with a superb list of Tasmanian drops, wandering occasionally across Bass Strait (like most Tasmanians) into Victoria and South Australia. Beers are mainstream; cocktails are more interesting. Love the cork-filled bar frontage. (📞03 6224 0611; www.grapebar.com.au; 55 Salamanca Pl; 🕐11am-11.30pm Sun-Thu, to 2am Fri & Sat)

Local Life

Old-school Pubs

There are so many new craft-beer joints, cocktail spots and cafe-bars around here it's hard to know where to start. For a more down-to-earth beer experience, follow perplexed-looking locals into an old-school waterside pub: try the **Telegraph Hotel** (☑ 03 6234 6254; www.facebook.com/telegraphhotel; 19 Morrison St; ⊙ 11am-late) or Customs House Hotel (p53), both on Morrison St.

Entertainment

Peacock Theatre

29 ⭐ Map p54, C8   THEATRE

This intimate theatre (165 seats) is inside the artful Salamanca Arts Centre (p56), along with a handful of other small performance spaces. Hosts theatre, dance, music and film. (☑ 03 6234 8414; www.salarts.org.au/venue/peacock-theatre; 77 Salamanca Pl; ⊙ box office 9am-5pm)

Federation Concert Hall

30 ⭐ Map p54, D1   CLASSICAL MUSIC

Welded to the Hotel Grand Chancellor, this concert hall resembles a huge aluminium can leaking insulation from gaps in the panelling. Inside, the Tasmanian Symphony Orchestra does what it does best.

(☑ 1800 001 190; www.tso.com.au; 1 Davey St; ⊙ box office 10am-4pm Mon-Fri)

Irish Murphy's   LIVE MUSIC

31 ⭐ Map p54, A7

Pretty much what you'd expect from any out-of-the-box Irish pub: crowded, lively, affable and dripping with Guinness. Free live music of varying repute from Tuesday to Sunday nights (open-mic on Tuesday; originals on Wednesday). (☑ 03 6223 1119; www.irishmurphys.com.au; 21 Salamanca Pl; ⊙ 11am-late)

7D Cinema   CINEMA

32 ⭐ Map p54, B8

Something new for Hobart: quick-fire, short 3D film 'rides' where you sit on a moving simulator. No scheduled ticketing – just turn up and jump on the next ride. (☑ 03 6224 6825; www.7dcinema.com.au; 8 Montpelier Retreat; adult/child $14/12; ⊙ 10am-10pm Mon-Thu, 10am-late Fri & Sat, 10am-9pm Sun)

Shopping

Salamanca Market   MARKET

33 🔒 Map p54, C7

Every Saturday morning since 1972, the open-air Salamanca Market has lured hippies and craft merchants from the foothills to fill the tree-lined expanses of Salamanca Place with their stalls. Fresh organic

Tasmanian honey at Salamanca Market

produce, secondhand clothes and books, tacky tourist souvenirs, ceramics and woodwork, cheap sunglasses, antiques, exuberant buskers, quality food and drink… It's all here, but people-watching is the real name of the game. Rain or shine – don't miss it! (☏ 03 6238 2843; www.salamanca.com.au; Salamanca Pl; ☺ 8am-3pm Sat)

Handmark Gallery ART

34 🔒 Map p54, C7

A key tenant at the Salamanca Arts Centre (p56), Handmark has been here for 30 years, displaying unique ceramics, glass, woodwork and jewellery, plus paintings and sculpture – 100% Tasmanian. (☏ 03 6223 7895; www.handmark.com.au; 77 Salamanca Pl; ☺ 10am-5pm)

Local Life
Friday Night Fandango

Some of Hobart's best live tunes get an airing every Friday night at the Salamanca Arts Centre Courtyard (p47). It's a free community event with the adopted name 'Rektango'. Acts vary month to month – expect anything from African beats to rockabilly, folk and gypsy-Latino. Drinks essential (sangria in summer, mulled wine in winter); dancing near-essential.

Art Mob

Kathmandu   SPORTS & OUTDOORS

35 🔒 Map p54, C8

Gear-up for your imminent Tasmanian bushwalking epic at this excellent outdoors store, founded in the 1980s by latter-day Tasmanian Jan Cameron (…who sold the business in 2006). (📞03 6224 3027; www.kathmandu.com.au; 16 Salamanca Sq; ⏱9am-5.30pm Mon-Thu, to 7pm Fri, to 5pm Sat, 10am-4.30pm Sun)

Wursthaus   FOOD

36 🔒 Map p54, B7

Follow your nose into this brilliant fine-food showcase just off Salamanca Place, selling speciality smallgoods, cheeses, cakes, breads, wines and pre-prepared meals. (📞03 6224 0644; www.wursthaus.com.au; 1 Montpelier Retreat; ⏱8.30am-6pm Mon-Fri, 8am-5pm Sat, 10am-5pm Sun)

Hobart Book Shop   BOOKS

37 🔒 Map p54, C8

Step into the hushed Hobart Book Shop, with its excellent array of reads and dedicated wall full of

Top Tip
Salamanca Market

If you're only going to be in Hobart for a few days, make sure one of them is a Saturday so you can check out Salamanca Market (p66), which has been filling trestle tables since 1972. Rain or shine it's an engaging experience, with as many things to eat and drink as buskers and things to buy. And unless you're going to get here at 6am, forget about finding a car park!

Tasmanian authorly efforts. (📞03 6223 1803; www.hobartbookshop.com.au; 22 Salamanca Sq; ⏱9am-6pm Mon-Fri, to 5pm Sat, 10am-5pm Sun)

Art Mob   ART

38 🔒 Map p54, E2

Gorgeous Aboriginal fine arts from around Australia have found their way to the Hobart waterfront. (📞03 6236 9200; www.artmob.com.au; 29 Hunter St; ⏱10am-6pm)

Explore

Northern Hobart

Hobart's northern suburbs are a real mix of tough working-class neighbourhoods and engaging cultural highlights. North Hobart itself is home to the city's most ebullient, bohemian restaurant and nightlife strip, strung along a sinewy stretch of Elizabeth St. Cafes, a cinema, pubs, craft-beer breweries, multicultural eats, live music venues – it's all here.

The Sights in a Day

There are of plenty of break-fast cafes to choose from in North Hobart: **Raincheck Lounge** (p85) and **Berta** (p82) are two of our faves. Later on, stretch out with a few low-key hours exploring the excellent **Royal Tasmanian Botanical Gardens** (p79) on the leafy **Queen's Domain** (p79). Alternatively, pick up a bike from **Spoke Bike Hire** (p80) and trundle north to MONA.

Back in North Hobart for lunch, head to **Burger Haus** (p80) and order something beefy, best consumed on the dinky terrace. Afterwards, promenade up and down the Elizabeth St strip: a lengthy browse in the **State Cinema Book-store** (p87) is near mandatory.

Time for a pre-dinner drink: for a glass of Tasmanian wine try **Willing Bros** (p85), or for craft beer temptations, swing into **The Winston** (p84). For dinner, bite off something meaty at classy **Roaring Grill** (p84), or dig into a divine curry at **Annapurna** (p82). As the night unfurls, an art-house film at the **State Cinema** (p86; pictured left) may entice, or perhaps a live band at the **Republic Bar & Café** (p86).

For a local's day in northern Hobart, see p76.

Top Sights
North Hobart (p72)

Local Life
North Hobart Streetwise (p76)

Best of Hobart

Eating
Sweet Envy (p81)

Roaring Grill (p84)

Drinking
The Winston (p84)

T-Bone Brewing Co (p85)

Willing Bros (p85)

Entertainment
Republic Bar & Café (p86)

State Cinema (p86)

Homestead (p86)

Getting There

🚗 **Car** Driving around North Hobart and the other northern suburbs is the easiest way to go.

🚕 **Taxi** Grab a cab to the North Hobart restaurants then back to your accommodation.

🚶 **Walk** Explore the North Hobart strip on foot.

🚌 **Bus** Route 551 runs from central Hobart to North Hobart.

Top Sights
North Hobart

North Hobart (or 'NoHo' to those with a sense of humour), for decades one of Hobart's poorer suburbs, is now a hip enclave with soaring real-estate prices and new-found bohemian soul. The Elizabeth St strip sustains dozens of restaurants and at least one watering hole for every night of the week. Add Hobart's best cinema and live-music venue to the mix and you've got one seriously potent little neighbourhood.

◉ Map p78, A3

The Winston (p84)

Eating in NoHo

Hungry? Head straight to North Hobart (do not pass Go, do not collect $200). Bounded by Federal St to the North and Burnett St to the south, the buzzy 'NoHo' strip along Elizabeth St has something for all tastes, from a spiffy steakhouse grill to Indian, Italian, Asian, Thai, Mexican, Turkish, tapas, burger joints, kebab shops, bakeries, cafes, patisseries, espresso nooks… The vibe here is relaxed and earthy, the antithesis of the flashier waterfront scene. Most restaurants here are BYO (bring-your-own alcoholic drinks, sometimes wine only), and you'll generally feel comfortable wearing jeans and a T-shirt. The scene is fast-changing: new businesses are opening all the time, steadily occupying new shops south of Burnett St as options diminish on the main strip. If you wanted tangible evidence of Hobart's emerging rep as a foodie haunt, here it is!

Time for a Drink?

In between all the North Hobart eateries you'll find a clutch of places to wet your whistle – some crammed with cool youngsters and savvy wine drinkers, some resolutely old-school and home to a species of old boozehound you don't see too often in Hobart these days. Top spots for a drink include **The Winston** (p84), a scruffy craft-beer pub at the northern end of the strip; the **Republic Bar & Café** (p86) at the southern end (also Hobart's best live-music room); the wine bar **Willing Bros** (p85); and **Room For A Pony** (p85), a spacious former petrol station doing good things with local wine and spirits. And if you are into propping up the bar (or just read a lot of Charles Bukowski), ask someone to point you towards the Queen's Head or the Crescent Hotel.

☑ Top Tips

▶ Parking can be tight around Elizabeth St, but there's a big car park behind the stores off Burnett St (once servicing a now-closed neighbourhood super-market).

▶ Book ahead at most restaurants here: it's a popular precinct.

▶ Running late and no time for a pre-movie drink? Don't fret: at the State Cinema (p86) you can take a glass of something good into the theatre with you.

✖ Take a Break

The North Hobart restaurant strip along Elizabeth St is one big break waiting to be taken. For coffee and cake the artful **Sweet Envy** (p81) is unbeatable.

For a tasting flight of crafty brews in the afternoon try **T-Bone Brewing Co** (p85).

Sweet Envy (p81)

Understand

Tangles

Legendary Australian cricketer and all-round good guy Max Walker (1948–2016), nicknamed 'Tangles' for his zany (but highly effective) bowling style, grew up in North Hobart. His father, Max senior, ran the big red-brick Empire Hotel – now the Republic Bar & Café (p86) – on the corner of Elizabeth and Burnett Sts, and Max junior was a regular interference underfoot at the bar. Aside from claiming 138 wickets in 34 international cricket test matches at an average of 27.47, Tangles was also a trained architect, a writer (14 books!), a TV presenter, public speaker, professional footballer (he played VFL football with the Melbourne Demons before he became a pro cricketer) and father of five kids. So raise a glass to Tangles – an irrepressible Tasmanian character – as you catch a live band at the Republic today.

Live Music

You can occasionally spy a sneaky busker twanging a guitar in the shadows here, but a more viable live-music option is the Republic Bar & Café. Formerly the staunch red-brick Empire Hotel, the Republic now hosts the pick of the Australian and international touring acts that visit Hobart (those not big enough to sell out a stadium), with local original acts filling out the gaps in the schedule. Great food and beer complete the package. The Winston also has regular live music, as does the rangy Homestead bar (country, folk, blues and cheap beers), a little further down Elizabeth St.

Art-house Cinema

Feel like a flick? The plush State Cinema (p86) at the upper end of the Elizabeth St strip is an old-timey theatre (1913) that's been turned into an art-house miniplex, with eight snug screening rooms, a rooftop screen for nights when Hobart's weather gods are feeling charitable, plus a bar, a cafe, and the fabulous State Cinema Bookstore (p87), where the selection of books on art and cinema is predictably good.

○ Local Life
North Hobart Streetwise

The North Hobart strip – at its essence the 500m stretch of Elizabeth St between Federal St to the north and Burnett St to the south – has evolved over the past decade into Hobart's alternative food and drink hub. It's an effervescent place, night or day, with dozens of multicultural places to eat and a new breed of craft-beer and wine bars complimenting old-school pubs. Hobart's best cinema and live-music venue are here too.

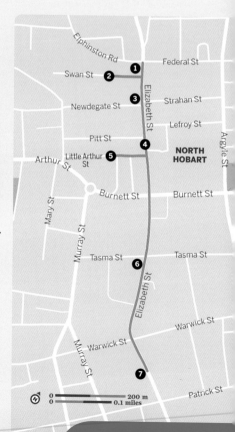

❶ North Hobart Post Office

What a beauty! A bright architectural spark at the top of the Elizabeth St strip, the ornate 1920s North Hobart Post Office is totally endearing. Painted handsomely in burgundy, cream and forest-green, it's a locally cherished building. It's enough to make you want to write a letter.

❷ Swan St

North Hobart was traditionally one of Hobart's edgier working-class enclaves – home to hard-drinking, hard-fisted hombres employed at the zinc factory at nearby Lutana. Some of the streets around here you'd probably avoid walking down, given the choice. Swan St was one such avenue: check out the gorgeous redbrick Victorian houses along its southern flank.

❸ North Hobart Pubs

North Hobart was complicit in the city's rampant booziness in colonial times, and despite the advent of craft beer, there are still some old-time pubs here. Try the **Queens Head Hotel** (400 Elizabeth St), hanging tough in the thick of the action; or the **Crescent Hotel** (100 Burnett St), around the corner.

❹ Hungry? Of Course You Are

Eating-out is North Hobart's *raison d'etre*. Walking down Elizabeth St you'll be spoilt for choice, with dozens of options vying for your hunger: Indian stalwarts, Mexican upstarts, Italian interlopers, brilliant bakeries and cool cafes. Excellent!

❺ Little Arthur St

A little pedestrian alleyway runs west off Elizabeth St and becomes Little Arthur St, a photo-worthy laneway with some of North Hobart's oldest workers' cottages on one side, and (sadly) a car park and fat bank of ugly brown-brick 1980s townhouses on the other. Worth a look.

❻ South of Burnett St

A western urban inevitability: suburbs gentrify, become hip, rents rise, and new businesses need to think laterally to get a foothold. So it is with North Hobart: shopfronts on the main strip are at a premium. Thinking outside the box, new restaurants, bars and cafes have seeded themselves south of Burnett St, extending the NoHo scene downhill. Sub-Burnett trailblazers include **T-Bone Brewing Co** (p85), **Capulus Espresso** (p82) and **Amici Italian** (p82).

❼ Shambles Brewery

In an un-obvious location midway between the main North Hobart action and the CBD is the excellent **Shambles Brewery** (☎03 6289 5639; www.shamblesbrewery.com.au; 222 Elizabeth St, North Hobart; ☺noon-late Wed-Sun). Shambles is notable for its slick interior design, excellent hoppy offerings and sense of humour (try the velvet-smooth Barry White porter).

GRANT DIXON / GETTY IMAGES ©

Conservatory at Royal Tasmanian Botanical Gardens

Sights

Royal Tasmanian Botanical Gardens

GARDENS

1 ⊚ Map p78, D1

On the eastern side of the Queen's Domain, these small but beguiling gardens hark back to 1818 and feature more than 6000 exotic and native plant species. Picnic on the lawns, check out the Subantarctic Plant House or grab a bite at the restaurant or cafe. Across from the main entrance is the site of the former Beaumaris Zoo, where the last captive Tasmanian tiger died in 1936. Call to ask about guided tours. (✆ 03 6166 0451; www.rtbg.tas.gov.au; Lower Domain Rd, Queen's Domain; admission free; ⊙8am-6.30pm Oct-Mar, to 5.30pm Apr & Sep, to 5pm May-Aug)

Queen's Domain

PARK

2 ⊚ Map p78, D1

When Hobart was settled, the leafy hill on the city's northern side was the governor's private playground, upon which no houses were to be built. Today the hillock is called the Queen's Domain and is public parkland, strewn with cricket, tennis and athletics centres, the Hobart Aquatic Centre (p80), native grasslands, lookouts and the Royal Tasmanian Botanical Gardens (p79). Pedestrian overpasses on the western side provide easy access to North Hobart. (☎ 03 6238 2886; www.hobartcity.com.au/recreation/queens_domain; via Tasman Hwy, Glebe)

Spoke Bike Hire
CYCLING

 3 Map p78, E4

Mountain bikes, hybrids, kids' bikes for hire, plus loads of advice on riding around the city and beyond. You can even hop on the bike track here and roll all the way to MONA (about 20km). (☎ 03 6232 4848; www.spokebikehire.com.au; 20 McVilly Dr, Cenotaph; bike hire per hour/day/2 days from $15/25/45; ⏰ 9am-5pm Sep-May, reduced hours Jun-Aug)

Top Tip
Urban Greenery

Hobart's northern suburbs can feel a bit hard-edged and bleak at times. For a leafy antidote, stretch your legs with Hobart's lunchtime jogging crew around the wide-open Cenotaph (p80) and hilly Queen's Domain (p79), or tag along with local pram-pushing families on a wander through the lush nooks and rolling riverside lawns of the Royal Tasmanian Botanical Gardens (p79).

Hobart Aquatic Centre
SWIMMING

 4 Map p78, D4

The excellent Hobart Aquatic Centre at the foot of the Queen's Domain offers recreational moisture, even when it's raining. Inside are leisure pools, lap-swimming pools, a spa, a sauna, a steam room, gym, aqua aerobics, and regular aerobics for landlubbers. (☎ 03 6222 6999; www.hobartcity.com.au/recreation/the_hobart_aquatic_centre; 1 Davies Ave, Glebe; adult/child/family $7.50/5/20; ⏰ 6am-9pm Mon-Fri, 8am-6pm Sat & Sun)

Cenotaph
MONUMENT

 5 Map p78, E4

Part of the broader Queen's Domain, this epic monument forms a visual finishing point if you look down the *looong* axis of Macquarie St from South Hobart. It's actually a war memorial: there used to be soccer pitches mowed into the grass around its base, but things are a bit more respectful these days. (off McVilly Dr, Glebe)

Eating

Burger Haus
BURGERS $

 6 Map p78, A3

Blaring 1980s rock and boasting big beefy burgers and a little terrace on which to sit, chew and contemplate the

Cenotaph

moody hues of Mt Wellington...this place has got it all! The Haus Burger (with bacon, onion rings, caramelised pineapple and mustard mayo) reigns supreme. (📞03 6234 9507; www. theburgerhaus.com.au; 364a Elizabeth St, North Hobart; mains $10-16; ⏲11.30am-10pm)

Sweet Envy PATISSERIE, CAFE $

 7 Map p78, A3

A delicate diversion along North Hobart's restaurant strip, Sweet Envy conjures up gossamer-light macarons, madeleines and cupcakes, plus donuts, gourmet pies and sausage rolls (try the pork and fennel version) and fantastic ice creams and sorbets, all made on the premises.

Grab a scoop of bad-ass 'Darth Vader' super-choc ice cream and hit the streets. (📞03 6234 8805; www.sweetenvy. com; 341 Elizabeth St, North Hobart; items $5-10; ⏲8.30am-5pm Tue-Sat)

Pancho Villa MEXICAN $$

 8 Map p78, A3

Cool renovation! A dour redbrick bank has become a super-moody tequila bar and restaurant (Day of the Dead skulls, pressed metal lanterns), where you order selections from the menu – creative tacos, enchiladas, quesadillas and corn and bean dishes – and knock them back with the aforementioned white spirit. 'Pancho Sundays' consume the courtyard:

$5 tacos and tequila shots; $30 cocktail jugs (forget about work tomorrow…). (☏03 6234 4161; www.panchovilla.com.au; cnr Elizabeth & Pitt Sts, North Hobart; items $7-15; ⏱5.30pm-late Mon-Wed, 11.30am-3.30pm & 5.30pm-late Thu-Sun)

Annapurna INDIAN $$

 9 Map p78, A3

It seems like half of Hobart lists Annapurna as their favourite eatery (you'd better book). Northern and southern Indian options are served with absolute proficiency: the *masala dosa* (south Indian crepe filled with curried potato) is a crowd favourite. Takeaways, too. Hard to top. (☏03 6236 9500; www.annapurnaindiancuisine.com;

Local Life
New Coffee Cool
Hobart's streets sustain a hip new breed of pop-up coffee carts and hole-in-the-wall coffee shops. In North Hobart, you can get a slice of tart, a bit of cake or a biscuit at low-tech **Capulus Espresso** (☏0459 661 001; www.facebook.com/capulusespresso; 271 Elizabeth St, North Hobart; items from $3; ⏱6am-4pm Mon-Fri, to noon Sat), a coffee nook behind a roller door just south of the NoHo strip. But what you're really here for is the coffee – outstanding hot black stuff. Check out the kooky hairdresser through the back door.

305 Elizabeth St, North Hobart; mains $16-18, banquets $22-32; ⏱noon-3pm & 5-10pm Mon-Fri, 5-10pm Sat & Sun;)

Amici Italian ITALIAN $$

 10 Map p78, A3

Mighty fine pasta, calzones and pizzas in a corner-shop restaurant that manages to feel more sophisticated than the menu, which still feels the need to include a Hawaiian pizza and a dedicated 'gourmet pizza' section (admittedly, very nice). The fettuccine marinara is hard to beat. (☏03 6234 7973; www.amicirestaurant.net.au; 310 Elizabeth St, North Hobart; mains $23-36; ⏱5-9pm Tue-Sun)

Vanidol's ASIAN $$

11 Map p78, A2

A pioneering North Hobart restaurant, Vanidol's has a diverse menu that travels effortlessly around Asia with dishes including spicy Thai beef salad, Nepalese lamb curry and Balinese chicken. Expect a well-thumbed passport full of vegetarian dishes, too. Also in South Hobart (p115). (☏03 6234 9307; www.vanidols-north-hobart.com; 353 Elizabeth St, North Hobart; mains $18-30; ⏱5.30pm-late;)

Berta CAFE $$

12 Map p78, A3

Atmospheric NoHo cafe with perfect people-watching window seats, pressed-tin ceilings, classy cafe

FON THACHAKUL / SHUTTERSTOCK ©

fare and a wine list travelling from Tasmania to Tuscany. Kick-start your morning with five-grain porridge with cinnamon crumble; for lunch try the pistachio-crumbed calamari with chickpeas, parsley and harissa mayo. (☑03 6234 4844; www.bertahobart. com.au; 323a Elizabeth St, North Hobart; mains $13-28; ⊙8am-3.30pm Mon-Fri, to 4pm Sat, to 2.30pm Sun)

Pasha's
TURKISH $$

13 Map p78, B4

More interesting than your average Turkish eatery, the Pasha's menu incorporates the expected Ottoman goodies – pide, dolma, kofta – plus a few more surprising dishes. Try the *sukuk:* grilled Turkish sausage with garlic yoghurt, tomato and spinach. Takeaway Turkish dips, too. (☑03 6234 6300; www.facebook.com/pashas turkishrestaurant; 216 Elizabeth St, North Hobart; mains $15-34; ⊙11am-late Tue-Sat)

All Thai
THAI $$

14 Map p78, A3

Straight-up, reliable Thai offerings on the North Hobart strip – orange-and-black colour scheme, clattery chairs and a busy vibe. Check the blackboard for daily specials (fingers crossed for the stir-fried crispy pork belly in homemade curry paste).

IMAGE COURTESY OF T-BONE BREWING CO.

T-Bone Brewing Co

(☏ 03 6234 8113; www.allthai.com.au; 333 Elizabeth St, North Hobart; mains $17-24; ⏱ 5.30-9pm Mon-Thu & Sun, to 9.30pm Fri & Sat; 🖉)

Roaring Grill   STEAK $$$

Named for the 'Roaring 40s' winds that sweep across these southern latitudes, sassy Roaring Grill (see 9 ✖ Map p78; A3) plates up the best Tasmanian fish and meat. It's a stylish split-level fit-out – exposed brickwork, dark wood tables and globular glassware – a far remove from the old foam mattress shop that was here for as long as anyone can remember.

(☏ 03 6231 1301; www.roaringgrill.com; 301 Elizabeth St, North Hobart; mains $27-35; ⏱ 5pm-late Mon & Tue, noon-late Wed-Sun)

Drinking

The Winston   PUB

15 🍺 Map p78, A2

The grim old art deco Eaglehawk pub has been transformed into the Winston, a hipster-driven, US-style craft-beer alehouse. Grab a pint of the house stout from one of the beardy guys behind the bar and check out the wall of US registration plates near the pool table. Calorific bar food and live music, too. (📞03 6231 2299; www.thewinstonbar.com; 381 Elizabeth St, North Hobart; ⏱4pm-late)

T-Bone Brewing Co
CRAFT BEER

16 🚇 Map p78, B3

Obsessively brewed real ales steal the show at this new North Hobart brew-bar, a stylish black beer-bunker reviving an old corner shop, just a short wobble from the main Elizabeth St action. Sit by the fold-back windows, or play peek-a-boo with the beer vats, bubbling beyond a hole in the wall. Tasting flights $16. (📞0407 502 521; www.tbonebrewing.com.au; 308 Elizabeth St, North Hobart; ⏱4pm-late Wed & Thu, 2pm-late Fri-Sun)

Willing Bros
WINE BAR

17 🚇 Map p78, A3

Hey – a classy wine bar! Just what NoHo ordered. Pull up a window seat at the front of the skinny room and sip something hip from the tightly edited menu of reds, whites and bubbles. Food drifts from Moroccan fish cakes to spicy lamb *empanadas* – perfect fodder for a post-movie debrief. (📞03 6234 3053; www.facebook.com/willingbros; 390 Elizabeth St, North Hobart; ⏱3pm-late Tue-Sun)

Room For A Pony
BAR

18 🚇 Map p78, A3

There's more than enough room for a pony at this converted petrol station – you could fit a whole herd on the concrete terrace out the front (soon to be grassed ... with outdoor stage!). Stop by for a Chinese chilli omelette or a burger (mains $11 to $20), a glass of wine, or a local-spirits cocktail (the rhubarb sour is a killer). (📞03 6231 0508; www.roomforapony.com.au; 338 Elizabeth St, North Hobart; ⏱7am-late Mon-Fri, 8am-late Sat & Sun)

Local Life

Trailblazing Cafe

A trailblazing North Hobart cafe (here long before all the hype), **Raincheck Lounge** (📞03 6234 5975; www.rainchecklounge.au; 392 Elizabeth St, North Hobart; tapas $6-19, mains $9-22; ⏱7am-7pm Mon-Fri, 7.30am-3pm Sat & Sun) is an enduring slice of urban cool. Raincheck's bohemian room and street-side tables see punters sipping coffee, reconstituting over big breakfasts, and conversing over generous tapas such as broccolini with anchovy crumb, or chorizo in peperonata. There's a decent wine list and sassy staff to boot.

Entertainment

Republic Bar & Café

LIVE MUSIC

19 ⭐ Map p78, A3

The Republic is a raucous art deco
pub hosting live music every night
(often free entry). It's the number-
one live-music pub around town,
with an always-interesting line-up,
including international acts. There
are loads of different beers and
excellent food (mains $24 to $36; try
the Jack Daniels–marinated scotch
fillet!). Just the kind of place you'd
love to call your local. (☑03 6234
6954; www.republicbar.com; 299 Elizabeth
St, North Hobart; ⊙11am-late; 🛜)

State Cinema

CINEMA

20 ⭐ Map p78, A2

Saved from the wrecking ball in
the 1990s, the multiscreen State
(built in 1913) shows independent
and art-house flicks from local and
international film-makers. There's
a great cafe and bar on-site, plus
a rooftop screen, a browse-worthy
bookshop (p87) and the foodie temptations of North Hobart's restaurants
right outside. (☑03 6234 6318; www.
statecinema.com.au; 375 Elizabeth St, North
Hobart; ⊙10am-late Mon-Fri, 9.30am-late
Sat & Sun)

Homestead

LIVE MUSIC

21 ⭐ Map p78, B4

This old pub has been here forever
under myriad names: never a particularly successful or enduring
business venture. But the rambling
Homestead seems to be making a
better fist of things, with live country, blues, folk and sundry singer-
songwriters. Cheap pints Tuesday;
cheap jugs Wednesday. (☑03 6234
4589; www.facebook.com/thehomesteadtas;
304 Elizabeth St, North Hobart; ⊙4pm-late
Tue-Sun)

The Winston (p84)

Shopping

State Cinema Bookstore
BOOKS

Wander through a hole in the wall from the artful State Cinema (p86) into the 1883 building next door (see 20 ⭐ Map p78: A2), to discover a wonderful world of words, pages and pages with words on them. Art, architecture, travel, biography and film (all the good things) are the mainstays. (✆03 6234 6318; www.statecinemabookstore.com.au; 373 Elizabeth St, North Hobart; ⊙10am-5pm Sun-Thu, 10am-late Fri & Sat)

Top Sights
MONA

Getting There

⚓ MR-1 from Brooke Street Pier

🚗 Via Brooker Hwy (11km)

🚌 MONA shuttle bus from the city or airport

🚲 20km from the city

MONA – the brilliant, notorious, challenging Museum of Old & New Art in Hobart's northern suburbs – is a very unusual place, and not just because it's founded/funded by an eccentric gambling millionaire. It's also more fabulously unhinged, sexy, renegade, offbeat, puerile and intelligent than any other art museum you might care to mention. Look, feel and think: that's the MONA effect.

Monanism

'Monanism' is the name given to the broad collection of art here, numbering upwards of 1900

View of MONA from the Derwent River

pieces. Not all of these are on display, but works are rotated regularly to keep things (more) interesting. Some works are so big and/or important that the museum was designed around them, including *Snake,* a 46m-long array of images exploring the connections between myth and modernity; and the *Chamber of Pausiris,* containing the coffin and mummy of a 2000-year-old Egyptian. Other must-sees include the room dedicated solely to the worship of Madonna; the fabulous *bit.fall,* a programmed waterfall that spells out words as it descends; and every kid's favourite, the impressive poo machine *Cloaca Professional,* which recreates (with alarmingly accurate waste products) the human digestive system.

For an insight into MONA's incredible architecture, check out www.mona.net.au/museum/architecture – an entertaining interview with the architects, explaining the thinking behind the design and the rather amazing site.

The O

At MONA there aren't any plaques on walls or dimly lit pasted-up A4 explanations of what you're looking at. And it is dimly lit in here! You're going to need some kind of guide to get you through.

The solution is 'The O' – essentially an iPod with headphones, issued for free, loaded-up with all kinds of art info that you can either listen to and accept, read and forget, or dismiss outright. Content is classified into 'Art Wank', 'Gonzo', 'Ideas' and 'Interviews', putting various spins on what you're seeing, including (often hilarious) commentary from David Walsh and the artists themselves.

The O is also interactive – hit the 'love' or 'hate' icons to give a little vox-pop feedback. If

Museum of Old & New Art

☏ 03 6277 9900

www.mona.net.au

655 Main Rd, Berriedale

adult/child $25/free, Tasmanian residents free

🕙10am-6pm daily Jan, 10am-6pm Wed-Mon Feb-Apr & Dec, 10am-5pm Wed-Mon May-Nov

☑ Top Tips

▶ Some of the stuff at MONA is ... well, pervy. If you blush easily, ask which naughty rooms to avoid. Ditto if you're strobe-averse.

▶ MONA is open every day in January (the rest of the year, Tuesday is staff sleep-in day).

✗ Take a Break

Grab a coffee and quick-fire bite at the museum cafe, or for a more refined experience, try the **Source** (mains $22-38; 🕙7.30-10am & noon-2pm Mon, Wed, Thu & Sun, 7.30-10am, noon-2pm & 6pm-late Fri & Sat) restaurant for lunch or dinner.

Understand
MONA Goes Gothic

When the winter solstice creaks around in June, **Dark MOFO** (www.darkmofo.net.au; ⏰Jun) stirs in the half-light. This moody festival – featuring live music, installations, readings, film noir and midnight feasts, all tapping into Hobart's edgy gothic undercurrents – has grown in popularity to rival the city's long-running New Year's festival scene. Locals rug-up, drink red wine around bonfires, talk, argue and eat, ruminating over the macabre and the unexpected.

Much less disquieting is the summertime **MONA FOMA** (MOFO; www.mofo.net.au; ⏰Jan), MONA's Festival of Music & Art, featuring eclectic musical offerings curated by a high-profile 'Eminent Artist in Residence' (EAR). Previous EARs have included John Cale, Ava Mendoza and Nick Cave. Stirring stuff.

you want to use your own iPhone you can download The O app (free wi-fi at the museum). Afterwards, you can have the details of your visit (as recorded by The O) emailed to you, so you can relive your MONA experience at home.

Exhibitions
As well as the main Monanism collection, MONA also hosts regular exhibitions digging up the dirt on specific subjects. In 2016 there was 'Hound in the Hunt', an experimental installation by artist Tim Jenison involving a distressingly simple method of recreating 17th-century art with mirrors; and 'On the Origin of Art', exploring how art, like the desire for food, sex or to protect our children, is hard-wired into our biology. Exhibitions cost extra, as you'd expect; book online.

Moorilla & Moo Brew
Before there was MONA, there was **Moorilla** (☎03 6277 9960; www.moorilla.com.au; tastings/tours $10/15, redeemable with purchase; ⏰tastings 9.30am-5pm Mon-Wed, tours 3.30pm Wed-Mon), a winery started in 1962 by Claudio Alcorso (1913–2000), an Italian with a keen eye for architecture and an even better eye for a good grape. Now MONA runs Moorilla: you can taste some at the cellar door, drink some at the on-site bars and restaurants, or take a winery tour at 3.30pm Wednesday to Monday ($15, bookings essential).

MONA's **Moo Brew** (www.moobrew.com.au; $15; ⏰tours 12.45pm Fri) has been around since Hobart's hipsters were beardless and too young to obsess about craft beer. Quality offerings include a pilsner, hefeweizen, dark ale and pale ale, brewed in nearby Bridgewater. As with the Moorilla wines, you can taste some at MONA's cellar door, drink some on-site, or take a one-hour tour out at the brewery, starting every Friday at 12.45pm ($15; bookings required).

Stairwell inside the museum

Understand
Bonus MONA

MONA is enough of a tourist lure in itself... but wait, there's more!

After swanning through the exhibits inside MONA, check out the excellent little **MONA Shop** (⊙10am-6pm daily Jan, 10am-6pm Wed-Mon Feb-Apr & Dec, 10am-5pm Wed-Mon May-Nov) near the entry, selling quirky, interesting and disarming gifts for the folks back home, plus excellent art books (pick up a copy of *A Bone of Fact*, the hefty 2014 autobiography of cashed-up MONA founder David Walsh).

On the lawns at MONA in late summer through the autumn, the savvy **MONA Market** (⊙11am-4pm Sun Feb-Apr) is a predictably off-the-wall event, with live music, street performers and quality arts-and-crafts stalls.

Finally, for a slice of luxury, book one of the private, uber-chic **MONA Pavilions** (d from $700; P ✳ 🛜 ⛵). These eight modern, self-contained chalets (one- and two-bedroom) are equipped to the nines, with private balconies, wine cellars, river views and oh-so-discreet service. An indoor swimming pool is an essential aid to relaxation, and MONA itself is in your backyard.

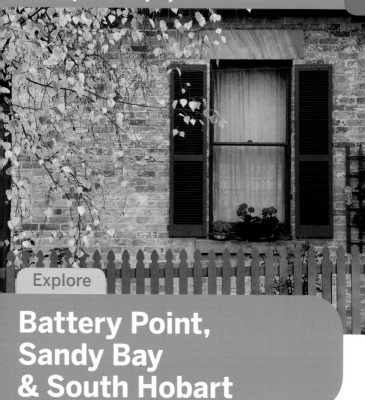

Explore

Battery Point, Sandy Bay & South Hobart

This broad southern swath is backed by looming Mt Wellington (*kunanyi* to the Muwinina people), the Battery Point headland jutting into the Derwent River. Battery Point was Hobart's first 'neighbourhood' and today hosts a photogenic clutch of old houses, cafes and B&Bs. Next door is affluent Sandy Bay, with atmospheric South Hobart nooked in below the mountain: both have excellent eateries.

The Sights in a Day

☀ Wake up! Coffee time! Head to busy Sandy Bay Rd and order a strong one at hip little **Sash Coffee** (p103). For something more solid, wander up to Hampden Rd in Battery Point (take cute little Billy Goat Lane off Quayle St) and choose a cafe – **Milli Vinilli** (p104) is a quirky option. Afterwards, the engaging **Narryna Heritage Museum** (p101) is nearby – an insight into domestic life in old Hobart Town.

☀ The little streets and heritage architecture or **Battery Point** (p94) itself demand an afternoon's exploration. The spire of **St George's Anglican Church** (p101) will peek into view from most places in the precinct. For a unique look at the neighbourhood from the water, sign up for a paddle with **Roaring 40s Kayaking** (p102).

☾ There's not much going on nocturnally in Battery Point, but grab a pre-dinner beer at **Preachers** (p108) or the old **Shipwright's Arms Hotel** (p108). Head back to Sandy Bay for dinner: **Don Camillo** (p107) has been here for decades, and is still plating-up Hobart's best Italian. For a more relaxed Italian experience, try **Solo Pasta & Pizza** (p104).

For a local's day in Battery Point, see p98.

Top Sights

Battery Point (p94)

◯ Local Life

Battery Point Backstreets (p98)

💗 Best of Hobart

Historic Atmosphere

Battery Point (p94)

Shipwright's Arms Hotel (p108)

Narryna Heritage Museum (p101)

Eating

Jackman & McRoss (p102)

Don Camillo (p107)

Parks, Gardens & Viewpoints

Princes Park (p99)

Napoleon St Playground (p99)

Roaring 40s Kayaking (p102)

Getting There

🚗 **Car** BYO car is the way to go (though Battery Point parking is hellish).

🚶 **Walk** Walk to Battery Point from the city or Salamanca Place.

🚌 **Bus** For Sandy Bay take bus 402 or 429 from the city. For South Hobart, bus 446, 447, 448 or 449.

Top Sights
Battery Point

An empty rum bottle's throw from the water-front, the old maritime village of Battery Point is a tight nest of lanes and 19th-century cottages, packed together like shanghaied landlubbers in a ship's belly.

This harbourside 'hood oozes history – a visit here is a window into Hobart's colonial soul. First designated as farm land by Hobart's settlers, Battery Point was soon rezoned as residential: hundreds of little sailors' and whalers' cottages soon sprang up, built in eave-less Georgian style, plus larger homes built for

Map p100, D2

www.batterypoint.net

merchants and sea captains. Today, cafes, galleries and B&Bs prevail.

Historic Highlights

Take a walk down Kelly St for a good look at some traditional, working-class Battery Point cottages; then spin around Arthur Circus – a sweet little circular street around a village green with a chestnut tree and a set of swings in it. The brick cottages here are typical of early Battery Point, built for soldiers from the local garrison. More affluent Battery Point mansions pop up along Mona St and the lower end of Hampden Rd.

You wouldn't know it these days, but Battery Point's residents didn't always maintain impeccable standards of behaviour (rum, sailors and prostitutes – what could possibly go wrong?). When the time came to repent, St George's Anglican Church (p101) on Cromwell St was the place to be. Designed by colonial architect John Lee Archer, this noble spire (1838) sits atop the highest point of the neighbourhood like a candle on a cake, and is visible from right across southern Hobart. It also served as a beacon for returning sailors, navigating their way up the misty Derwent River estuary.

For a condensed and highly authentic window into colonial life, pay a visit to **Narryna Heritage Museum** (p101) on Hampden Rd. This 1837 sandstone house is crammed with domestic remnants form Battery Point's early days.

Hampden Rd Scene

If Battery Point has a 'spine', Hampden Rd is it, a slender, sinewy thoroughfare that runs the length of the suburb, linking Sandy Bay Rd at one end with Castray Esplanade at the other. Along its length are most of Battery Point's commercial endeavours, including some good

☑ Top Tips

▶ Aside from some good restaurants, there's not much shakin' in Battery Point after dark. Plan on retreating to Salamanca Place.

▶ Parking here is as bad as it gets in Hobart: tight little streets with no driveways are a bad combo for drivers. Ditch the wheels and walk instead.

✗ Take a Break

Hampden Rd sustains a string of good cafes and restaurants: Jackman & McRoss (p102) is surely Hobart's best bakery-cafe.

For a sneaky drink, head to the hidden-away Shipwright's Arms Hotel (p108) on Colville St, with its timeless sea-going vibes.

accommodation, a pub, a museum, some gift shops and some excellent cafes and restaurants. If you're out exploring the 'hood for a day, you'll probably find yourself drawn back here a couple of times for a coffee, some lunch or an afternoon glass of wine. Top of your list should be Jackman & McRoss (p102), a brilliant bakery-cafe that few would argue is Hobart's best; Ristorante Da Angelo (p104) for an early pizza dinner; and Magic Curries (p104), purveyors of Hobart's best Indian offerings. The multi-talented Milli Vinilli (p104) is also worth a look for an all-day breakfast, Japanese bento box, a glass of vino or a free apple with your takeaway coffee.

Understand
Where's the Battery?

The suburb's namesake gun battery was built in 1818 on the promontory overlooking the Derwent River, cannons aimed out towards prospective invading Americans, Russians, French, Dutch or whomever else might have had the gall to attack old Hobart Town and claim it as their own. The invasion never happened, the guns were dismantled and the site of the old battery – in Princes Park on the end of Hampden Rd – is now interred beneath a kids' playground.

Fancy a Beer?

Just off Hampden Rd at the Sandy Bay Rd end is Preachers (p108), a nooked-away bar in a historic cottage, with a laid-back beer garden. One of Hobart's first purveyors of fine craft beer, it's an eccentric spot for a cold one…and even has a ghost!. The **Prince of Wales Hotel** (☎ 03 6223 6355; www.princeofwaleshotel. net.au; 55 Hampden Rd, Battery Point; r incl breakfast $85-160; P 🛜), a short walk away on the corner of Hampden Rd and Kelly St, is a 1960s red-brick incursion, incongruously modernist in its design, but old enough now to invoke a certain sense of nostalgia.

Hidden Battery Point

Walking around Battery Point, it's often the little hidden places and surprising things that beguile and endear. You'll indeed need to be goat-like to traverse Billy Goat Lane and Nanny Goat Lane – steep, skinny flights of steps linking Quayle St with St Georges Tce on the Sandy Bay side of the suburb.

Another hidden gem is the little waterside Purdon Featherstone Reserve off Derwent Lane at the foot of Trumpeter St, named after some local boat builders. From here you can view Battery Point's last remaining boat yards and moorings. The unusual contemporary house on the right as you descend to the park was built for the founder of

Hampden Road, Battery Point

Incat (International Catmarans) – a latter-day Hobart boat-building success story.

Sometimes it's the more transient occurrences in Battery Point that give the neighbourhood its character: a little pile of seashells on a doorstep; gentle little river waves splashing onto the tiny beach at the bottom of Finlay St; the stencil graffiti poem on the wall of the Shipwright's Arms Hotel (p108), which reads: *'Three flag-swept days/Ships monstrous and transitory/Heroes I could not captain'*.

Local Life
Battery Point Backstreets

Time-travel back into Hobart's colonial history with a walk around Battery Point. This was where the city's first farm was established, followed by military installations (the 'battery'), rows of compact sailors' cottages and estimable mansions built for wealthy merchants. History is everywhere here: a few hours exploring the backstreets is time well spent.

❶ Hampden Rd Cafes

Don't attempt anything without coffee and pastries. From Sandy Bay Rd, walk down Hampden Rd, Battery Point's photo-worthy commercial strip, and check yourself into one of the cafes here. Pull up a footpath table if it's sunny, get a feel for the village atmosphere and fuel-up for your walk ahead.

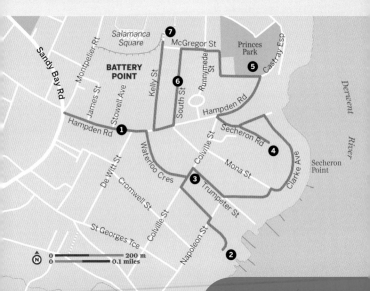

② Battery Point Shipyards

It's something of a surprise to discover that Battery Point still has working shipyards, congregating around the lower end of Napoleon St. To get here, follow the arc of Waterloo Cres (Napoleon, Waterloo…we sense a theme emerging), cross Colville St and dogleg down Sloane St. Cast an eye over proceedings from the lovely little Napoleon St Playground.

③ Shipwright's Arms Hotel

From Napoleon St, walk back up to Colville St where you'll find one of the sources of Battery Point's traditionally boozy rep – the old **Shipwright's Arms Hotel** (p108), which has been serving beers to seagoing types since 1846. Duck inside and check out the maritime paraphernalia on the walls.

④ Secheron House

Walk down Trumpeter St, turn left onto Marine Tce then cast an eye up Mona St to see some of Battery Point's more impressive houses. Follow Clarke Ave around to Secheron Rd, where the National Trust–listed Secheron House (1831) resides in colonial splendour – the most lovely of Battery Point's heritage mansions. Peek through the gates: it's a private home these days.

⑤ Princes Park

Back on Hampden Rd, head downhill to Princes Park, where Battery Point's 'battery' once stood – a gun installation built in 1818 to protect Hobart from the threat of invading warships crewed by rival European powers. The cannons here were part of a network of 12 defensive sites around the Derwent River, and pointed seawards until 1878. Princes Park is now perfectly peaceful…although you can still see the stone entrance to the old magazine (ammunition storage area) under the park, where men once gathered to gamble and drink until the archway was barred shut in 1934.

⑥ South St

Compact little South St has an inexplicably good vibe. In itself the street is unremarkable – a lane-like thoroughfare crowded with old timber and stone cottages that aren't particularly consistent or in particularly good condition. But South St just oozes charm – the essence of Battery Point.

⑦ Kelly's Steps

At the bottom of Kelly St are **Kelly's Steps** (Kelly St, via Salamanca Pl, Hobart), named after one-time Hobart harbourmaster James Kelly. Built in 1839, the steps traverse the quarry face between Battery Point and Salamanca Place, which until their construction was impassable. Kelly himself (1791–1859) was a real go-getter, who fathered 10 children and outlived seven of them. From here the Salamanca Place bars are a short hop away – toast your Battery Point tour with a cold one or three.

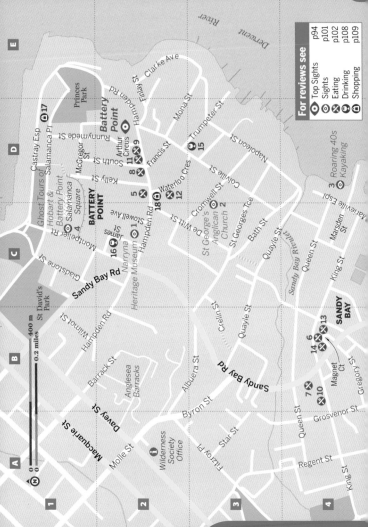

For reviews see	
◉ Top Sights	p94
◎ Sights	p101
⊗ Eating	p102
⊗ Drinking	p108
⊕ Shopping	p109

HEMIS / ALAMY STOCK PHOTO ©

Narryna Heritage Museum

Sights

Narryna
Heritage Museum   MUSEUM

1 ⊙ Map p100, C2

Fronted by a babbling fountain, this stately Greek-revival sandstone mansion (pronounced 'Narinna') was built in 1837 by trader Captain Andrew Haig. Set in established grounds it's a treasure trove of domestic colonial artefacts, and is Australia's oldest folk museum. (☎03 6234 2791; www.tmag.tas.gov.au/narryna; 103 Hampden Rd, Battery Point; adult/child $10/4; ⊙10am-5pm Tue-Sat)

St George's
Anglican Church   CHURCH

2 ⊙ Map p100, C3

Designed by colonial architect John Lee Archer, this landmark church (1838) sits atop the highest bit of land in Battery Point – visible from all over southern Hobart, and from out on the river (returning sailors would use it as a beacon). (☎03 6223 2146; www.stgeorgesbatterypoint.org; 30 Cromwell St, Battery Point; ⊙9.15am-2.15pm Tue-Fri, service 10am Sun)

Roaring 40s Kayaking

KAYAKING

3 Map p100, D4

Hobart is perhaps at its prettiest when viewed from the water. Take a safe, steady, 2½-hour guided paddle with Roaring 40s, named after the prevailing winds at these latitudes. You'll cruise from Sandy Bay past Battery Point and into the Hobart docks for some fish and chips while you float, before returning to Sandy Bay. (📞0455 949 777; www.roaring40skayaking.com.au; Marieville Esplanade, Sandy Bay; adult/child $90/60; ⏰10am daily Oct-Apr, plus 4pm Nov-Mar)

Ghost Tours of Hobart & Battery Point

WALKING

4 Map p100, C1

Walking tours of Battery Point oozing ectoplasmic tall tales, departing the 7D Cinema on Montpelier Retreat at dusk most nights. Bookings essential, and no kids under eight. At the time of writing their city-centre tour was being re-invented. (📞0467 687 004; www.ghosttoursofhobart.com.au; adult/child $25/15)

Eating

Jackman & McRoss

BAKERY $

5 Map p100, D2

Make sure you stop by this neighbourhood bakery-cafe, even if it's just to gawk at the display cabinet full of delectable pies, tarts, baguettes and pastries. Early-morning cake and coffee may evolve into a quiche for lunch, or perhaps a duck, cranberry and walnut sausage roll. Staff stay cheery despite being run off their feet. The city **branch** (📞03 6231 0601; 4 Victoria St, Hobart; ⏰7am-4.30pm Mon-Fri) has parallel prices. (📞03 6223 3186; 57-59 Hampden Rd, Battery Point; items $4-14; ⏰7am-5pm Mon-Sat)

Liv-eat

CAFE $

6 Map p100, B4

Soups, grilled salads, rolls, sandwiches, wraps, juices and smoothies – all of it fresh and/or made on the spot, and none of it deep-fried. It's a healthy formula not necessarily in accord with the lifestyles of the craft-beer fans who seem to flock here. Maybe it's the

Local Life

World Heritage South Hobart

In 2010 Unesco inscribed 11 Australian convict sites onto its register of places of 'outstanding universal value'. Tasmania contains five of these sites, including South Hobart's Cascades Female Factory Historic Site (p114), off Cascade Rd, where female convicts (25% of transportees) were imprisoned and put to work in miserable conditions.

Ristorante Da Angelo (p104)

good coffee they're after ... (☎ 03 6224 1999; www.liveat.com.au; 15 Magnet Court, Sandy Bay; mains $7-14; ☺ 6am-8.30pm; ♿)

Sash Coffee
CAFE $

 7 Map p100, B4

This urbane little caffeine crevice in the main bank of Sandy Bay shops has a few stools out the front and awesome plates of brioche French toast with banana, lemon curd and vanilla ice cream. The house fruit-and-nut loaf is fab, too. Oh, and kickin' coffee! (☎ 0449 799 664; www.facebook.com/sashcoffee; 1/163 Sandy Bay Rd, Sandy Bay; mains $8-12; ☺ 6am-5.30pm Mon-Fri, 7am-5pm Sat & Sun)

 Top Tip

Battery Point Access
Oddly, Battery Point can seem a bit difficult to access from Salamanca Place and the waterfront – there's a huge cliff in the way! (Salamanca Square was once a quarry). To get there via a sneaky shortcut, duck down a little alleyway at the eastern end of Salamanca Place and dogleg up Kelly's Steps (signposted), a sandstone stairway built in 1839 to navigate the precipice.

Ristorante Da Angelo

ITALIAN $$

8 Map p100, D2

An enduring (and endearing) Italian *ristorante*, Da Angelo presents an impressively long menu of homemade pastas, veal and chicken dishes, calzones, and pizzas with 20 different toppings. Colosseum images and Carlton Football Club team photos add authenticity. Takeaway, BYO and open late. (☏ 03 6223 7011; www.daangelo.com; 47 Hampden Rd, Battery Point; mains $17-35; ⏱5pm-late)

Magic Curries

INDIAN $$

9 Map p100, D2

There's a photo on the wall here of the Indian cricket team's visit in 2004 – a while ago, we know, but if it's good enough for Anil Kumble, it's good enough for us. Sip a Kingfisher beer in the magically coloured

Top Tip

Hobart Weather

If you're planning on getting out and about, Hobart is in fact the second-driest Australian capital city (after Adelaide). That's not to say it isn't cold! The weather here is highly changeable, too, so be prepared for any conditions in any season, wherever you are in the city.

interior and await your face-meltingly hot beef vindaloo. Excellent vegetarian options; takeaway available. (☏ 03 6223 4500; www.magiccurries.com.au; 41 Hampden Rd, Battery Point; mains $18-20; ⏱5-9pm; ☏)

Solo Pasta & Pizza

ITALIAN $$

10 Map p100, B4

The brilliant pastas, pizzas, risottos and calzones at Solo have been drawing hungry hordes for decades. Not that you'd know its age from looking at it: the snazzy glass-fronted room backed by racks of wine is almost futuristic. (☏ 03 6234 9898; www.solopastaandpizza.com.au; 50b King St, Sandy Bay; mains $10-26; ⏱5-10pm Tue-Sun)

Milli Vinilli

CAFE $$

11 Map p100, D2

So, Rob and Fab are running a cafe/wine bar in Battery Point now? Actually, no, and referencing these fake popsters certainly seems a questionable decision ... but Milli Vinilli is always busy! Opt for an upmarket toasted sandwich, a Japanese bento box, an all-day breakfast, or some evening tapas and a glass of local wine. Free apple with your takeaway coffee. (☏ 03 6224 1447; www.millivinillicafe.com; 45 Hampden Rd, Battery Point; tapas $12-21, mains $15-19; ⏱8am-3pm & 5-10pm Wed-Sun)

Understand

Hobart Gothic

Hobart is a uniquely fated town, crossed with a gothic, otherworldly spirit that seems to hang in the cobweb corners of the latitude. People have suffered here – indigenous Tasmanians and convicts – a grim legacy that can't be rewound or dismissed.

The Mountain & the Muwinina

Rising behind South Hobart is Kunanyi/Mt Wellington (p119) – *kunanyi* is the mountain's indigenous Muwinina name and it's often written with a lower case 'k' – its broad dolerite mass brooding and omnipresent in the icy wind. Beneath the mountain, a profound sense of loss and oblivion can bear down, and with it the thought that western civilisation should never have arrived.

Indeed, before the British arrived in 1803, the Muwinina lived here harmoniously for tens of thousands of years, maintaining a stable seasonal culture of hunting, fishing and gathering. In the early 1800s they watched from Kunanyi as the intruders cleared trees and built their city below. It's reasonable to consider that the first bloom of British sail cloth on the Derwent – and with it the guns, disease and alcohol that decimated Tasmania's Aboriginal population – has somehow cursed this place.

Convicted

Then came the convicts. Around 70,000 British criminals were sent to Tasmania up until the 1850s and locked in prisons so inhumane that today, among their ruins, the sense of sadness is palpable. The Port Arthur Historic Site southeast of Hobart is the prime example: even on sunny days the vibe here is grim (not helped by memories of the 1996 massacre here, when a lone gunman killed 35 people).

Back in South Hobart, the Cascades Female Factory Historic Site (p115) was where female convicts were incarcerated and made to work in vile conditions. Children suffered here, too: convict women sent to work on settler's farms would often return pregnant, give birth to their illegitimate children, then try desperately to keep them alive. It's said that when the Hobart Rivulet floods at the end of Degraves St, the bones of children sometimes wash loose among the dirt.

St George's Anglican Church (p101)

Understand
In Like Flynn

Legendary swashbuckling actor Errol Flynn was born in Battery Point, first showing his handsome, future-moustachioed face at the Queen Alexandra Hospital on Hampden Rd on 20 June 1909. Flynn lived in Hobart, where his father was a professor of biology, until he was sent to school in London at the rather pivotal age of 14. Flynn went on to become a swashbuckling Hollywood superstar – lighting up the screen in films like *Captain Blood* and *The Adventures of Robin Hood* – and a notorious ladies' man (hence the phrase 'In Like Flynn'), before expiring prematurely at age 50 whilst visiting Canada.

Three Japanese
JAPANESE $$

12 ✕ Map p100, D2

Run by (you guessed it) three Japanese friends, this mod little black-and-white restaurant sources its produce as much as possible from organic producers around southern Tasmania: mushrooms from Cygnet, pork from the Huon Valley, vegetables from Bagdad ... Try the Wagyu rice bowl, and scan the collection of soy and sake bottles at the front counter on your way out. (✆03 6224 1606; www.threejapanese.com.au; 38 Waterloo Cres, Battery Point; mains $18-26; ⏱5.30-9.45pm Wed-Sun)

Me Wah
CHINESE $$

13 ✕ Map p100, B4

From the outside, Me Wah looks just like any suburban shopping-mall joint. But inside it's an elegant confection of chinoiserie, almost bordering on over-the-top. The food is equally stellar, including terrific ways with seafood and world-famous-in-Hobart yum cha sessions from 11am on weekends. (✆03 6223 3688; www.mewah.com.au; 16 Magnet Ct, Sandy Bay; mains $19-40, tasting menu per person $135; ⏱noon-2.30pm & 6-9.30pm Tue-Sun)

Don Camillo
ITALIAN $$$

14 ✕ Map p100, B4

Just about the oldest restaurant in Hobart, little Don Camillo has been here forever and is still turning out a tight menu of classic Italian pastas, risottos and meat dishes (try the house-made ravioli). Look for the red Vespa parked out the front. (✆03 6234 1006; www.doncamillorestaurant.com; 5 Magnet Ct, Sandy Bay; mains $25-36; ⏱6-9pm Tue-Sat)

Understand
Whales in the Derwent

In the 1830s Hobartians joked about walking across the Derwent River on the backs of whales and complained about being kept awake at night by whales cavorting offshore. A glance across the river from from Battery Point or Sandy Bay might reveal any number of spouting blowholes and splashing flukes. In typical Tasmanian style, the ensuing whaling boom was catastrophic, driving local populations of southern right and humpback whales to near extinction. Though still endangered, the occasional forgiving whale returns to the Derwent during June-July northbound and October-November southbound migration. If you spy one, call the Parks & Wildlife Service whale hotline on ☎0427 WHALES (☎0427 942 537).

Drinking

Shipwright's Arms Hotel   PUB

15 🚇 Map p100, D3

Backstreet 'Shippies' is one of the best old pubs in town. Soak yourself in maritime heritage (and other liquids) at the bar, then retire to your clean, above-board berth upstairs or in the newer en-suited wing (doubles with/without bathroom $150/90). Other bonuses include hefty pub meals and the delight in saying you're having a drink on Trumpeter St. (☎03 6223 5551; www.shipwrights arms.com.au; 29 Trumpeter St, Battery Point; 🛜)

Preachers   BAR

16 🚇 Map p100, C2

Grab a retro sofa seat inside this 1849 sailmaker's cottage, or adjourn to the ramshackle garden bar – in which an old Hobart bus is now full of beer booths – with the hipsters. Lots of Tasmanian craft beers on tap, plus cool staff and a resident ghost! A steady flow of burgers and tapas keeps the beer in check. (☎03 6223 3621; www.facebook.com/ preachershobart; 5 Knopwood St, Battery Point; 🕙noon-late)

GERARD WALKER / GETTY IMAGES ©

Jackman & McRoss (p102)

Shopping

Despard Gallery   ART

17 Map p100, D1

Top-notch contemporary Tasmanian arts – jewellery, canvases, glassware and ceramics – in a lovely old sandstone building a short stroll from Salamanca Place. (☏03 6223 8266; www.despard-gallery.com.au; 15 Castray Esplanade, Battery Point; ⏱10am-6pm Mon-Fri, to 4pm Sat, 11am-4pm Sun)

On Hampden Creative   GIFTS & SOUVENIRS

18 Map p100, D2

Excellent little two-room Battery Point shop selling excellent little handmade Tasmanian things: jewellery, candles, soaps, scarves ... even pots of leatherwood honey and raspberry jam! (☏0414 518 739; 66 Hampden Rd, Battery Point; ⏱10am-5pm Mon-Fri, to 3pm Sat & Sun)

Top Sights
Cascade Brewery

Getting There

🚗 From the city take Davey St then dogleg onto Macquarie St, which becomes Cascade Rd – a 3.5km trip.

🚌 446, 447, 448 or 449 from the city centre.

Even for Aussies who don't drink beer (yes, there are a few), the name 'Cascade' is synonymous with Tasmania, and Hobart in particular. On the banks of the Hobart Rivulet in South Hobart, this is Australia's oldest brewery (1824) – and is a rather arresting piece of architecture to boot. Brewery tours have become an essential Hobart experience.

History & Architecture

Woah, check out that facade! It's fair to say that upon first sight, the towering Cascade building is more than a little spooky-looking, especially on a cold winter's day when there's snow on Mt Wellington and the sun doesn't reach into this wet corner of South Hobart for more than an hour or two.

From modest beginnings in 1832 when the first Cascade beer was sold (stemming from an original brewing operation set up in 1824), Cascade grew to monopolise beer sales in southern Tasmania by the 1900s. The brewery's marvellous facade dates from 1927, designed by local architects Glaskin and Ricards to build upon existing structures. The facade almost didn't make it past 1967, when devastating bushfires blazed through many Hobart suburbs and all but destroyed the brewery. But the thirsty Hobart community rallied and rebuilt Cascade: amazingly, the beloved brewery was pumping out beer again within three months.

Brewery Tour

Brewery tours leave from the visitor centre across the road from the iconic main brewery building. The main tour (what most people are here for) takes you into the factory workings to see how Cascade's beers are assembled from base ingredients: water, malt, hops and yeast. Be prepared to tackle a lot of stairs, which only serves to prime your thirst when it comes time to taste the product at tour's end. Tours last 90 minutes, departing four to seven times daily. Note that if you're here on a weekend, some of the brewery machinery may not be running.

☑ 03 6212 7800

www.cascadebrewery.
com.au

140 Cascade Rd, South Hobart

brewery tours adult/child 16-18yr $30/15, Cascade Story tour adult/child $15/5

⏱ tours daily

☑ Top Tips

▶ Tour numbers are limited: book in advance (online).

▶ Tour safety rules: no booze beforehand; no loose jewellery; legs must be fully covered; only enclosed, flat shoes.

✗ Take a Break

One of Hobart's best cafes is nearby **Ginger Brown** (☑ 03 6223 3531; 464 Macquarie St, South Hobart; mains $10-20; ⏱ 7.30am-4pm Mon-Fri, 8.30am-4pm Sat & Sun; 🖉 🐾) – perfect for a quick lunch.

The Cascade Hotel (p133) is a resolutely old-school South Hobart boozer.

Visitor Centre

Understand
Hobart Rivulet Track

If the sun is shining (and/or perhaps you've had too many beers to drive), you can walk to/from the brewery along the easygoing 2.7km Hobart Rivulet Track, following the waterway from the brewery down to Molle St on the edge of the Hobart CBD. See www.greaterhobarttrails.com.au/track/hobart-rivulet-park for details.

All-Ages Experiences

Aside from the main brewery tour (for folks aged 16 and over), there are two other tours that the whole family can enjoy (no tastings or factory access).

Cascade Story A garden tour running for 45 minutes, looking at the history of the brewery, brewing in Hobart more generally, and highlighting some of the characters who've played a part in Cascade's evolution. Tours run once daily, four days a week during school holiday periods – usually Tuesday and Friday to Sunday.

In the Shadow Historical Play

A dramatic re-enactment of the life and trials of Sophia Degraves, wife of Cascade founder Peter Degraves (was he casting a shadow over Sophia, or was it Mt Wellington?). Tours run once daily, three days a week – Monday, Friday and Saturday – and last 45 minutes.

Summer Jazz

A further enticement at Cascade is the Summer Jazz Festival, a series of outdoor gigs on the lawns at the brewery visitor centre, every Sunday afternoon from early December to the end of February. Kick back on a rug and sip your way into the local product to a smooth bee-bop and zah-ba-de-bah soundtrack.

> ### Understand
> ### Peter Degraves
>
> Back in 1824, the Cascade Brewery's founder was one Mr Peter Degraves – a visionary and a bullish businessman, certainly, but also a bankrupt and convicted thief who served time in Hobart for his crimes. Nearby Degraves St is named after him.

JOHN SONES SINGING BOWL MEDIA / GETTY IMAGES ©

Actors in 'In the Shadow'

Top Sights
Cascades Female Factory Historic Site

Getting There

🚗 Degraves St in South Hobart is the extension of McRobies Rd, which itself off Macquarie St.

🚌 446, 447, 448 or 449 from the city centre

For more than a century most Hobartians lived in blissful ignorance about this storied South Hobart convict site, reduced as it was to crumbling walls, weed-filled yards and sundry outbuildings purloined into other uses. Recently listed by Unesco as a site of major historic significance, this former female prison is now high on the 'must-see' list of many visitors to Hobart.

Tasmania's Female Convicts

It's a rather staggering fact that one in four convicts sent to Van Diemen's Land from Britain – around 12,500 between 1803 and 1853 – was female. So grim was life in the UK for unmarried, uneducated, impoverished young women that many of these transportees committed deliberate crimes in order to be sent to the other side of the planet, hoping that their lives would somehow improve – could they be any worse? Unfortunately, for many who ended up at the Female Factory in South Hobart, which opened in 1828 on the site of a failed distillery, the answer was 'yes'.

Convict Life for Women

The Female Factory wasn't just a prison, it was also a work house and a processing plant for sending women out into the colony as (essentially) slave labour for affluent settlers.

Classified into three groups based on the seriousness of their misdemeanours, women were put to work cooking, sewing, laundering and spinning wool for up to 12 hours a day, often in freezing, wet conditions. Any insubordination was punishable by close, solitary confinement in darkened cells. Sleeping conditions were cramped, often with 600 women crammed into a facility designed for 200.

Those sent out to work in the colony faced a different menace. Land and estate owners often saw the provision of sexual favours as part of the contract between them and their servants. Many women, unable to conceal their resultant pregnancies for very long, would be returned to the Female Factory and labelled as shameful sinners. Many illegitimate children were born here, with many of them succumbing to the cold, wet, louse-ridden living conditions.

📞 03 6233 6656

www.femalefactory.org.au

16 Degraves St, South Hobart

adult/child/family $5/5/15, tour $15/10/40, 'Her Story' dramatisation $20/12.50/60

🕒 9.30am-4pm, tours hourly 10am-3pm (except noon), 'Her Story' dramatisation 11am

☑ Top Tips

▶ Beat the crowds: get in early for the 10am Heritage Tour.

▶ You can visit the site without taking a tour, but the Heritage Tour ($10) and 'Her Story' re-enactment ($20) really help with interpretation.

✖ Take a Break

For a pan-Asian lunch or dinner, swing into the excellent Vanidol's (📞 03 6224 5986; www.vanidolsouth.com; 361a Macquarie St, South Hobart; mains $15-22; 🕒 11am-2pm & 5.30-9pm Tue-Sat).

Understand
On the Town

- - - - - - - - - - - - - - - -

A common misconception about
female convicts transported to
Van Diemen's Land is that they
were mostly prostitutes being
punished for their profession.
Convict ship records would label a
prisoner as 'on the town' if indeed
they had been a prostitute, but
this term was also applied to
vagrant transportees who'd been
living on church benefaction.
Percentages of convicts listed as
'on the town' generally ranged
between 20% and 40%.

Interpreting the Past

When convict transportation to
Van Diemen's Land ceased in 1853,
the Female Factory was slowly
wound down, eventually closing in
1877. It's a measure of how much
shame Tasmanians have heaped on
their convict past that so little of
the Female Factory's original built
fabric remains. Much of the complex
was demolished, carted away, sold
off and built over, or just left to
crumble. You can enter the site and
look around without taking a tour,
but as the remains are so scant, a
tour is the best way of interpreting
what you see.

CASCADES FEMALE FACTORY: IMAGE COURTESY OF

Tours & Experiences

Forty-five-minute guided **Heritage Tours** run seven days a week at 10am, 11am, 1pm, 2pm and 3pm, regardless of what the weather sees fit to provide (on a wet winter morning the atmosphere here is palpably grim). Guides shed light on the site's remaining and demolished built structures, and give some insights into punishment, work and reform at the 'factory'.

A dramatic re-enactment of life here in 1833 can be experienced with **Her Story** (☑ 03 6233 6656, 1800 139 478; www.livehistoryhobart.com.au; 45min tour adult/child $20/12.50), with two costumed actors playing out various roles. It's a moving, time-shifting insight into the convict existence, sincerely and authentically played

out. The show lasts 45 minutes and runs at noon daily, except for Saturdays during the winter months (June to August).

> Understand
> ## Female Convict Research Centre
>
> Think you might have convict blood from a femme crim of days long gone? Check out www.femaleconvicts.org.au, run by the affiliated Female Convict Research Centre, to dig into your past. The website is also a font of info on convict ships, administrative processes and institutions.

Top Sights
Kunanyi/Mt Wellington

Getting There

🚗 Take Davey St from the city centre to Fern Tree, then Pinnacle Rd to the summit (19km).

🚌 448 (direct) or 447 or 449 (indirect) to Fern Tree

Known as *kunanyi* to the local Muwinina Aboriginal people, 1271m-high Mt Wellington is a serious chunk of stone. Dolerite, in fact, violently intruded between layers of older rock when Australia ripped itself away from Antarctica around 40 million years ago. These days Kunanyi is Hobart's beacon, its protector and its barometer...and the views from the top are awesome!

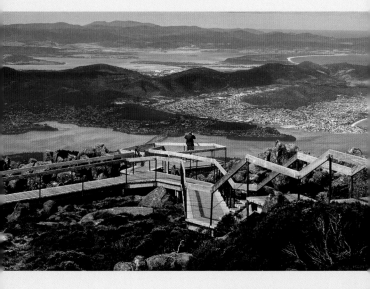

The Summit

The sealed 12km Pinnacle Rd from Fern Tree to the Mt Wellington summit was the brainchild of Albert Ogilvie, premier of Tasmania in the 1930s. When the Great Depression hit hard in Hobart, Ogilvie deemed that all those unemployed hands would be best engaged in doing something constructive for the community. After several years of backbreaking labour, Pinnacle Rd opened in 1937. Initially very visible from the city and not entirely popular, the road became know as 'Ogilvie's Scar'.

These days the road has mostly been obscured by trees; much more visible are the two huge transmission towers at the peak. There's a nifty little curvy-roofed viewing room here, too, in which you can shelter from the wind and check out the eye-popping views. A drive to the summit to assess the city below is now a near-mandatory Hobart experience. Don't be deterred if the sky looks overcast from sea level: often the summit rises above the gloom, and the view from the top extends across a magical sea of rolling white cloud-tops.

Hiking & Biking

The mountain is criss-crossed by numerous hiking paths, bike tracks, horse-riding trails and fire roads, some well-trodden and wide, some overgrown and intriguing. Popular tracks include the Radfords Track, Pinnacle Track, Fern Glade Track, the steep Zig Zag Track and the Organ Pipes track below Kunanyi's trademark cliffs. Check out www.greaterhobarttrails. com.au for detailed track and planning info. At any time on the mountain, expect rapid and extreme weather shifts: this ain't no walk in the park (well, it is, but you know what we mean – be prepared).

Mount Wellington

☎ 03 6238 4222

www.wellingtonpark.org.au

Pinnacle Rd, via Fern Tree

☑ Top Tips

▶ The fabulous www. wellingtonpark.org.au is a wealth of maps, history and bushwalking and mountain-biking info.

▶ Mt Wellington's weather is notoriously fickle: be ready for snow and 100km/h winds in December and warm sunshine and twittering birds in June.

▶ For Pinnacle Rd snow-closure updates see www.hobartcity. com.au.

✗ Take a Break

At forested Fern Tree, halfway up the hill, the rudimentary **Fern Tree Tavern** (☎ 03 6239 1171; www.facebook.com/ ferntreetavern; 680 Huon Rd, Fern Tree; ⊙11am-10pm Tue-Sun) has cold beer and warm fires.

Understand
The Springs

About half way up Pinnacle Rd is a place called the Springs, where once stood a popular hotel and health spa. The verandah-wrapped 'Hotel Mount Wellington' opened in 1907 – a lavish, two-storey Victorian timber chalet, with 16 guest rooms, hot and cold running water, and drawing, sitting, dining and smoking rooms. Sadly the hotel, like many other buildings and huts on the mountain's lower flanks, was destroyed by Hobart's devastating 1967 bushfires. These days, **Lost Freight** (📞0417 719 856; www.lostfreight.com.au; Pinnacle Rd, via Fern Tree; items $3-6, 9am-4pm Tue-Fri, 9am-4.30pm Sat & Sun, reduced winter hours) fills the Springs' hospitality niche – a cool little container warming up passing mountaineers.

For an excellent mountain-bike experience, tackle the **Mt Wellington Descent** (📞1800 064 726; www.underdownunder.com.au/tour/mount-wellington-descent; adult/child $75/65; ⏰10am & 1pm daily year-round, plus 4pm Dec-Feb). Take a van ride to the summit, then enjoy 22km of super-scenic downhill cruising (mostly – the last 5km are flat) on a mountain bike. It's terrific fun, with minimal energy output and maximum views! Tours start and end at 4 Elizabeth St on the Hobart waterfront (near the visitor information centre), and last 2½ hours.

Winter Snow

Sure, Canberra has sub-zero nights and Melbourne requires one to don a woolly hat occasionally, but do any Australian cities other than Hobart have access to ACTUAL SNOW!? 'No', is the resounding response. Mt Wellington wears a white cloak for most of the winter (June to August), with snowfalls often reaching down into the suburbs. Local kids grow up knowing what it's like to build a snowman, hurl a snowball and pile a snow mound on the car bonnet for the ride back to sea level, watching in anticipation for the moment it melts and slides off onto the road.

Lost World

A real local secret (not so secret now, eh?), Lost World is an amazing boulder field near the peak of Mt Wellington, backed by a miniature version of the famous Organ Pipes dolerite cliffs below the summit, further to the south. Rock climbers, boulder-hoppers and bushwalkers venture here to lose a few hours in surreal solitude, to check out the views, or to play hide-and-seek among the massive fractured hunks of stone.

To get to Lost World, take the little track heading north from the car park at 'Big Bend', 9km up Pinnacle Rd from Fern Tree – the last major hairpin bend before the summit. It's a 45-minute walk one-way.

Pinnacle Rocks

Organ Pipes rock formation

Understand
Famous & Infamous Visitors

In February 1836 the esteemed naturalist Charles Darwin sailed into Hobart and set out to scale Mt Wellington. Darwin was intrigued by the mountain's geology and flora, vividly describing the sunny day he spent here in his book *The Voyage of the Beagle*.

A less savoury character was bushranger Rocky Whelan, who lived in 'Rocky Whelan's Cave', a short walk from the Springs. Whelan was an escaped convict who'd done hard time in Sydney, on Norfolk Island, and finally in Van Diemen's Land, where, upon his eventual recapture, he admitted to murdering a dozen men.

The Best of
Hobart

Taste of Tasmania festival (p144)
RICHARD I'ANSON / GETTY IMAGES ©

Best Walks
Hobart History Lesson

🏃 The Walk

As Australia's second-oldest capital city (we won't mention No.1, but it starts with 'S'), Hobart is riddled with interesting remnants of the 1800s. The waterfront, Battery Point and Salamanca Place are where it's at (or rather, where it was at 200 years ago). Sandstone is everywhere, literally the building blocks of a colony, hacked out of cliff faces around the city and still looking photogenic, particularly in Hobart's honey-coloured evening light.

Start Macquarie St

Finish Salamanca Place

Length 3km; three hours

🍴 Take a Break

As you wander over to the Henry Jones Art Hotel on Hunter St, duck into the in-house café **Jam Packed** (☎ 03 6231 3454; www.thehenryjones.com; Henry Jones Art Hotel, 27 Hunter St, Hobart; mains $10-25; ⏰ 7.30am-5pm; 📶) for a rejuvenating coffee shot.

JOYCE MAR / SHUTTERSTOCK ©

Tasmanian Museum & Art Gallery (p48)

❶ Macquarie St

Hobart's grand boulevard, Macquarie St trucks past many of the city's classic old sandstone buildings, including **St David's Cathedral** (p31), dating from 1868, the 1906 **General Post Office** and the 1864 **Town Hall**, with a design based on Palazzo Farnese in Rome

❷ Tasmanian Museum & Art Gallery

Not only is '**TMAG**' (p48) a fabulous cache of historic Tasmaniana, the museum buildings themselves are also really old. Check out the cavernous Bond Store (1824), the Private Secretary's Cottage (1813), and the Commissariat Complex (1808), Tasmania's oldest public building.

❸ Henry Jones Art Hotel

Built over a long-since-buried isthmus to Hunter Island, the Hunter St warehouses mirror those in Salamanca Place across Sullivans Cove. The outstanding **Henry**

Jones Art Hotel (p53) is here, built inside the former IXL jam factory.

❹ Parliament House

Cross the swing bridge and fishtail across the waterfront, passing historic Victoria Dock, Constitution Dock and Watermans Dock. Tasmania's noble sandstone **Parliament House** (p52) (1840) is just across Murray St. Tours are available on days when parliament isn't mass debating.

❺ St David's Park

Resist the photogenic frontage of Salamanca Pl for now, turning right instead to detour through St David's Park, the site of Hobart Town's original cemetery. Check out the picturesque pergola and walls lined with relocated colonial gravestones.

❻ Battery Point

Cut through Salamanca Mews, jag right onto Gladstone St, left onto Kirksway Pl then right onto Montpellier Retreat, arcing uphill into **Battery Point** (p94), Hobart's oldest residential area. Duck into the Hampden Rd cafes and spin around the improbably quaint Arthur Circus.

❼ Salamanca Place

Bumble down **Kelly's Steps** (p99), an 1839 sandstone link between Battery Point and the redeveloped 1830s warehouses of **Salamanca Place** (p44), Hobart's food-and-drink epicentre. Enjoy!

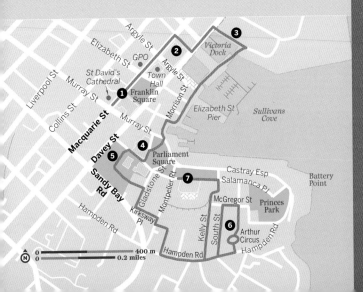

Best Walks
Hobart Pub Crawl

🏃 The Walk

Some cities in the world are great drinking cities (Dublin, Wellington, New Orleans, Buenos Aires...), and some cities just aren't (LA, Dubai, Singapore, Kuala Lumpur...). Lucky for you, Hobart falls squarely into the former category – a hard-drinking town that's been three sheets to the wind since the days of rum-addled soldiers in the barracks and sea-soaked whalers in the waterfront pubs. Many of the town's most atmospheric old boozers are still here: time to bend an elbow in a few.

Start New Sydney Hotel

Finish Shipwright's Arms Hotel

Length 2.5km; five hours

🍴 Take a Break

Nothing goes together quite as well as beer and pizza. Well, beer and curry, maybe... But for a fab Italian disc nearing the end of your pub crawl, try Battery Point's **Ristorante Da Angelo** (p104).

GRANT DIXON / GETTY IMAGES ©

New Sydney Hotel (p36)

① New Sydney Hotel

You have to applaud the confidence: Hobart's colonists may have viewed their city as the new version of Sydney, but it was never going to be as big. Revel in Hobart's 'boutique' scale at this atmospheric city **pub** (p36), with open fires, excellent beers and plenty of quiet corners in which to pursue the lost art of conversation.

② Brunswick Hotel

The **Brunswick Hotel** (p37) harks back to 1827 – allegedly Australia's second-oldest pub. A savvy architectural makeover exposes key bones in its old stone skeleton. Backpackers aplenty at the bar.

③ Hope & Anchor

If the Brunswick is Australia's second-oldest pub, the **Hope & Anchor** (p37) is the oldest! Licenced since 1807, if the walls here could talk it'd be a helluva loud conversation.

The upstairs dining room is festooned with amazing historical knickknacks.

4 Telegraph Hotel

Down on the waterfront, act like a longshoreman and mosey into this old art-deco **pub** (p66). Despite being afflicted by an infectious rash of 1990s turquoise tiles and corrugated iron, 'the Telly' still has boat-loads of charm.

5 Customs House Hotel

Across the road from Parliament House, the sandstone **Customs House Hotel** (p53) is in a prime waterfront position. Resisting the urge to hipster-fy itself, it's a determinedly old-school spot for a beer.

6 The Whaler

Formerly the much-adored Knopwoods Retreat, **The Whaler** (p64) is doing its best not to annoy anyone who might consider venturing back here

after the name change. Uncomplicated and open-to-all-comers, it's something of an anomaly on slick Salamanca Place.

7 Shipwright's Arms Hotel

When the Sydney to Hobart Yacht Race fleet sweeps into Hobart just prior to New Year's Eve, most of the yachties end up at **Shippies** (p108) – a classic backstreet Battery Point boozer that's been here since 1846. Whose shout?

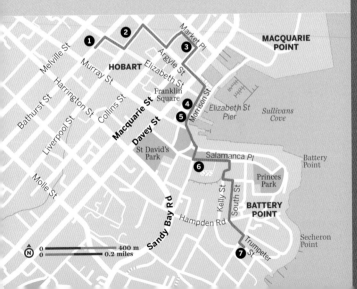

Best
Historic
Atmosphere

RICHARD CUMMINS / GETTY IMAGES ©

Hobart is endowed with more than its fair share of impressive (and at times, downright cute) historic buildings, many built with local sandstone that takes on a warm glow in Tasmania's soft southern light. Visiting Hobart's museums and walking around the city, the waterfront and Battery Point, it's easy to conjure up visions of days gone by.

Heritage Buildings

Hobart's amazing cache of well-cured old buildings makes it exceptional among Australian cities. There are more than 90 buildings classified by the National Trust here – 60 of them are on Macquarie and Davey Sts alone. The intersection of these streets features a gorgeous heritage sandstone edifice on each corner – the only instance of this in Australia – including the austere St David's Cathedral. Salamanca Place is of course a must-see; also worth a look is the 1864 Town Hall on Macquarie St – duck inside the lobby and have a look around.

Domestic Architecture

Hobart has been both cursed and blessed by Tasmania's stop-start economy. These days things are very much in the 'start' category, but often in the past local business sentiment has been catatonic at best. This economic lethargy, combined with a general lack of wealth in society, has been a blessing for Hobart's old houses: there just hasn't been enough money around to bulldoze old homes and build new ones. The net result? Hobart's stock of domestic architecture is now beautifully preserved. Georgian, Victorian, Edwardian, Federation, modern, mid-century…drive around the suburbs and play 'Name That Architectural Style'.

Best Historic Vibes

Battery Point Take a time-travelling stroll around the streets of Hobart's first neighbourhood. (p94)

Salamanca Place The marvellous old stone warehouses along Salamanca Place are utterly photogenic. (p44)

Henry Jones Art Hotel Built inside an old warehouse on Hunter St, this former jam factory is now an atmospheric boutique hotel. (p53)

Hope & Anchor Thirsty? Sit at the bar of Australia's oldest pub and soak up the vibes. (p37)

Shipwright's Arms Hotel Battery Point's maritime vibes reach fever pitch in this eccentric pub. (p108)

Hunter St warehouses (p53)

Best History Museums & Historic Sights

Cascades Female Factory Historic Site Hobart's female convicts lived, worked and died at this haunting South Hobart site. (p115)

Cascade Brewery It's not just about beer: the brewery itself is an imposing hark-back to old-time Hobart. (p111)

Tasmanian Museum & Art Gallery Aboriginal history, colonial heritage and the demise of the thylacine: just part of 'TMAG's broad historical remit. (p48)

Narryna Heritage Museum A window into the domestic lives of Hobart's colonial families. (p101)

Penitentiary Chapel Historic Site This spooky old chapel and prison complex on the city fringe is a disquieting place. (p30)

Hobart Real Tennis Club Built in 1875, this is one of only three 'Royal' tennis courts in the southern hemisphere. (p29)

Theatre Royal Australia's oldest working theatre runs guided tours … or catch a show! (p29)

 Worth a Trip

Drive out to the historic town of **Richmond** (population 1610), straddling the Coal River 27km northeast of Hobart. Once a strategic military post and convict station, the town is riddled with 19th-century buildings – it's arguably Tasmania's premier historic town. Businesses here do tend to err on the 'kitsch colonial' side of tourism, but it's certainly a picturesque little place. Day-trip bonus: the Coal River Valley wineries are en route.

Best
Eating

Eating in Hobart is one of the true pleasures of any visit down south. Local 'Mod Oz' (Modern Australian) restaurateurs are wide awake to southern Tasmania's excellent produce, and are doing good things with it in the city's kitchens. The cafe and coffee scenes here, too, will keep you wide awake, while seafood and pub-grub offerings are also reliably good.

Dining Destinations

Hobart's city centre proffers some excellent cafes and rapid-fire lunch venues, but when the sun sinks behind the mountain, there's not a whole lot going on here (with some notable exceptions). Instead, head for the waterfront and Salamanca Place, the epicentre of the city's culinary scene, where there's quality seafood everywhere you look.

Battery Point's Hampden Rd cafes and restaurants are always worth a look, while Elizabeth St in North Hobart (aka 'NoHo') has evolved into a diverse collection of cosmopolitan eateries: Indian, Asian, Mexican, cafes, patisseries, pubs... The Sandy Bay food scene is also bubbling along nicely (any suggestions for a cool nickname?).

Dinner Time?

Hobartians are big on breakfast and dinner, but lunch is something that sometimes morphs intro brunch or is squeezed in between other commitments. That said, a cafe breakfast isn't a daily event here – more of a weekend treat. A takeaway coffee is, however, a daily necessity for many folks.

It's probably something to do with that southern weather, but dinner happens early in Hobart: 6pm is a very reasonable hour to eat, and don't expect to arrive anywhere after 8.30pm and get a table.

Best Cafes

Jackman & McRoss This iconic Battery Point cafe is still going strong. Great staff and creative baking. (p102)

Sweet Envy As if the Elizabeth St strip in North Hobart wasn't sweet enough! Divine sweet treats. (p81)

Retro Cafe A pioneering Salamanca Place cafe in a prime spot for people watching. (p59)

Pilgrim Coffee Progressive pilgrim sets the pace in Hobart's downtown coffee scene. (p35)

Jackman & McRoss (p102)

Best Seafood & Steak

Flippers Super-fresh seafood to go, down on the waterfront (where the fish are). (p59)

Fish Frenzy Family-focussed seafood diner on the waterfront, with an eternally buzzy vibe. (p59)

Blue Eye High-end seafood at the far end of Salamanca Place. (p61)

Roaring Grill Roar into this North Hobart restaurant for a dose of island iron. (p84)

Astor Grill Classy city steaks and grills in a charming old brick building in the city centre. (p36)

Best Upmarket Dining

Don Camillo One of Hobart's first restaurants is still one of the best: superb Italian offerings in Sandy Bay. (p107)

Templo Templo sets the tempo on an unremarkable street, with entirely remarkable eats. (p34)

Aloft The best views in town from atop the Brooke St Pier. (p60)

Frank Frankly fabulous South American–inspired cuisine down on the waterfront. (p61)

Franklin Yet more 'Frank'-themed restaurant naming – this one is a stylish fit-out of an old newspaper factory. (p36)

Worth a Trip

About 3km north of the city centre, the stylish, light-filled **Cornelian Bay Boat House** (☏ 03 6228 9289; www.the boathouse.com.au; Queen's Walk, Cornelian Bay; mains $27-36; ⊙noon-2pm Sun-Tue, noon-2pm & 6-8.30pm Wed-Sat) restaurant-bar occupies a converted beach pavilion. The highly evolved menu features quality local produce, delivered with super service. Try the Boat House chowder, or the Scottsdale pork loin with cider-and-sage jelly.

Best
Pubs & Bars

Hobart's younger drinkers are 10,000 leagues removed from the rum-addled whalers of the past, but the general intentions remain true – drink a bit, relax a lot, and maybe get lucky and take someone home. Salamanca Place, the waterfront and North Hobart are the main drinking and nocturnal hubs.

GRANT DIXON / GETTY IMAGES ©

Pubs

Hobart once had so many pubs it was hard to walk more than a few hundred metres without being tempted into one for a quick ale. These days a lot of them around the city centre have closed (or been turned into backpacker hostels), with new craft-beer, whisky and cocktail bars the flavour of the decade. But you can still sniff out a few endearing old boozers here and there if you know where to look. Most pubs offer hefty traditional lunches from noon to 2pm, and dinners from 6pm to 8pm (young families get in early), plus open fires in the winter and occasional live tunes.

Bars

In a town renowned for drinking, it was just a matter of time before traditional all-things-to-all-people pubs gave way to more specialised booze rooms, dabbling in the dark arts of whisky, wine, cocktails and craft beers. These days there are plenty of hip little places where you can indulge your particular liquid whims, from dedicated wine bars to an emerging crew of craft-beer bars and moody outlets for fine Tasmanian whisky.

Best Traditional Pubs

Hope & Anchor Australia's oldest pub? Take up the discussion with the bar staff. (p37)

Shipwright's Arms Hotel Marvellously old-school backstreet pub in Battery Point. (p108)

New Sydney Hotel The best watering hole in the city centre has open fires, excellent food and interesting beers. (p36)

Brunswick Hotel CBD pub with a backpackers upstairs and dependable beers downstairs (backpackers and beer – a symbiotic relationship). (p37)

Best Craft-beer Bars

Winston Rootsy North Hobart epicentre for all things cold and crafty. (p84)

Preachers A raffish backstreet Battery Point brew bar full of student types…and a ghost! (p108)

Hobart Brewing Company Roll up, roll up: waterfront beers in the emerging Macquarie Point precinct. (p63)

T-Bone Brewing Co Nifty North Hobart

brew-bar just south of the main Elizabeth St strip. (p85)

Jack Greene Hunting-lodge vibes in Salamanca Place, with quality in the taps. Quality soloists keep the crowd attuned. (p63)

Best Wine, Whisky & Cocktails

Glass House The newest cocktail bar in town, with unbeatable river views and stylin' staff. (p63)

Willing Bros Uncork (or unscrew) a bottle of something luscious in North Hobart. (p85)

T-42° Enduring waterside classiness in the Elizabeth St Pier. (p63; pictured far left)

Grape Local, mainland and imported wines line the walls in this charming little cave. (p65)

Worth a Trip

Almost within eyeshot of the famous old Cascade Brewery just around the corner, the **Cascade Hotel** (☏03 6223 6385; www.cascadehotel.com.au; 22 Cascade Rd, South Hobart; ◷10am-late) in South Hobart has been pouring the local product since 1846. These days it's a reliable locals' hang-out with decent pub food (famously good steaks) and occasional live music, including free-wheeling jazz jams every Wednesday night.

Best
Entertainment

Some Hobartians come home in the evening, open a beer and sit and watch the sun set behind Kunanyi/Mt Wellington – what more entertainment do you need? A bit of live music, perhaps: Hobart is host to a clutch of good live-music pubs and a classical concert hall. The theatre scene simmers along here, too, and there are some top-notch sporting events to admire.

MICHAEL TAYLOR/GETTY IMAGES ©

Live Music

Hobart is big on drinking, and big on providing a live-music soundtrack to which you may drink. The bands that play the pub circuit here have long been mired in a cover-version cycle of doomed creativity – and compared to Melbourne or even Adelaide they still are. But the originals scene here is slowly gaining traction, and most nights of the week now you can hear something new and vaguely rockin'.

The live jazz scene here is much smaller, little trios and quartets sometimes popping up at waterfront bars (try Grape, IXL Long Bar or the Salamanca Whisky Bar). On the classical front, the Tasmanian Symphony Orchestra plays at the waterfront Federation Concert Hall.

Spectator Sports

Like to watch? In winter you can catch live Australian Football League (AFL; www.afl.com.au) games at Blundstone Arena in Bellerive on Hobart's eastern shore, with international and state cricket gracing the same venue in summer. Tennis fans look forward to the annual **Hobart International** (www.hobartinternational.com.au; ⏱Jan) womens' pro tournament every January (a prelude to the Australian Open in Melbourne).

Best Live Music

Republic Bar & Café Original rock, blues and folk acts most nights, both local and touring. (p86)

Brisbane Hotel Offbeat metal, punk, hip-hip and alt-rock in a city boozer that's been here forever. (p40)

Irish Murphy's Waterside Irish predictability, but with entertaining covers acts, open-mic nights and lots of originals. (p66)

Homestead A real mixed bag in North Hobart: folk, country, blues, zydeco, singer-songwriters ... and cheap beer! (p86)

Federation Concert Hall Highbrow classical on the waterfront, courtesy of the Tasmanian

Symphony Orchestra. (p66)

IXL Long Bar Regular live jazz in the old Hunter St warehouses. (p63)

Best Cinema

State Cinema A cornerstone of Hobart's artistic life, the arthouse State has eight screens, a cafe-bar and a bookshop. (p86)

MONA MONA has its very own cinema (of course it does) called Cinemona, screening arty recent releases and classics. (p89)

Best Theatre

Theatre Royal Australia's oldest theatre (1834) still has its old boards and actors treading on them. (p29)

Peacock Theatre An engaging program of theatre, dance, music and film in a cute little theatre off Salamanca Place. (p66)

Playhouse Theatre Long-running drama hub on Bathurst St in the city, producing musicals aplenty. (p40)

Worth a Trip

Hobart's home of cricket and football is **Blundstone Arena** (Bellerive Oval; ☎ tickets 13 28 49, tours 03 6282 0433; www.blundstonearena. com.au; 15 Derwent St, Bellerive). The North Melbourne Kangaroos AFL football club (www. afl.com.au) plays some home games here; international test, one-day and T20 cricket matches also pull crowds. Guided arena tours run at 10am on Tuesdays. The Tasmanian Cricket Museum is here, too.

North Melbourne Kangaroos at Blundstone Arena

Best
Parks, Gardens & Viewpoints

It's a legacy, perhaps, of Hobart's colonial history that this isn't what you'd call a 'leafy city'. The wilderness was the enemy in the 1800s: the only thing trees were good for was cutting down to build boats and houses. The flip-side of this clear-felling attitude is that there are some beautiful, manicured parks and gardens here (reproducing old England was conceptually easier for the colonists to handle). There are also some terrific vantage points around town, from which to eyeball this pretty city and it's ever-changing river and mountain.

Points of View

Hobart is so darn scenic, it's almost a prerequisite for houses to have a view of some sort: the river, the mountain, maybe both. With the notable exception of Sydney, most mainland Australian cities are aesthetically impoverished by comparison. Formal vantage points with pay-per-view binoculars, hotdog vans and oceans of car parking don't exist here: it's more a case of just driving around and seeing what you can see. There are views everywhere!

You won't find it in any tourist brochures, but for a classic view of Hobart and the Derwent River with the hulking mass of Kunanyi/Mt Wellington in the background, drive up to the local-secret lookout atop Rosy Hill on Hobart's eastern shore. The local council thoughtfully lops the tops off any trees that dare impede the view. To get here, cross the Tasman Bridge, head for Rosny, turn right at the lights onto Riawena Rd and follow the signs.

CLAUDINE VAN MASSENHOVE / GETTY IMAGES ©

Best Parks & Gardens

Royal Tasmanian Botanical Gardens Fourteen gorgeous hectares of immaculate lawns, exotic plant collections, greenhouses, fountains and ancient trees, some dating back to the late 1800s. (p79)

Princes Park Where once stood Battery Point's namesake gun battery is now this lovely park, with a fab kids' playground and lawns sloping down towards the river. (p99)

Cenotaph The Cenotaph itself is a towering war memorial, but the lawns surrounding it give Hobartians a much needed sense of wide-open space. (p80; pictured above)

View from Kunanyi/Mt Wellington (p118)

Queen's Domain Part of the Queen's Domain – the bulky hillock just to the north of the city – is consumed by Glebe, a sunny little suburb. The rest is semi-wilderness, cloaked in casuarinas, eucalypts and grasslands. (p79)

Napoleon St Playground This trim little park in Battery Point has a sunny patch of lawn for mum and dad to snooze on while the kids run amok. (p99)

Best Viewpoints

Kunanyi/Mt Wellington There's no denying Kunanyi – the big mountain is a key component of daily life in Hobart. And even if you drive half-way up Pinnacle Rd, the views over the city

and beyond are astonishing. (p119)

Victoria Dock For a picture-postcard view of Hobart, wander over to the north side of Victoria Dock on the waterfront and look back towards the city: fishing boats, office blocks and the marvellous mountain. (p53)

Roaring 40s Kayaking Grab an eyeful of Battery Point and the waterfront from the river on these excellent guided kayak paddles. (p102)

MONA ferry Don't bother driving to MONA: catch the ferry instead. Sip champagne in the 'Posh Pit' and assess the city and northern suburbs from the water. (p89)

 Worth a Trip

Kunanyi/Mt Wellington is irrefutably big, but if the summit is clouded over and you're still looking for a view, the old semaphore station atop **Mt Nelson** (352m) provides immaculate views over Hobart and the Derwent River. Drive up Davey St from the city, take the Southern Outlet towards Kingston and turn left at the top of the hill. Local buses 457, 458 and X58 also come here.

Best
Museums

Hobart is a really old town as far as white Australian history goes – only Sydney predates it. It follows, then, that the museums here are chock-full of interesting old things. And of course, Aboriginal history in the Hobart area goes back many tens of thousands of years – check out the Tasmanian Museum & Art Gallery for some engaging indigenous insights.

GRANT DIXON / GETTY IMAGES ©

MONA Much more than just a museum: MONA is an ethos, a philosophy, a way of life! Allow a full day here (at least): built-in eating and drinking venues will keep you fuelled up. (p89)

Tasmanian Museum & Art Gallery 'TMAG' has really lifted its game in recent years. This rather amazing collection of old buildings is now a must-visit Hobart experience. (p48)

Mawson's Huts Replica Museum Antarctica ain't that far away: see how the intrepid Sir Douglas Mawson coped with the cold in 1911. (p56)

Narynna Heritage Museum Hobart domestic life in colonial times is perfectly preserved at endearing Narynna, in Battery Point. (p101)

Maritime Museum of Tasmania Hobart and the sea are locked together for eternity. What the sea wants, the sea shall have … (p56)

Markree House Museum Markree House lifts the lid on Hobart between the wars (not quite mid-century modern, but almost as hip). (p31)

Allport Library & Museum of Fine Arts Adjunct to the State Library and beautifully bookish, this excellent little city museum is a trove of wonderful art. (p30; pictured above)

☑ Top Tips

In Hobart, history lives in the architecture, the streets and the landscape. Museums offer a mainline to the past, but some pre-trip reading will get your in the mood:

▶ *In Search of Hobart* (Peter Timms; 2009) Part social history, part contemporary critique.

▶ *In Tasmania* (Nicholas Shakespeare; 2004) A British spin on Tasmania's history and culture.

▶ *Thylacine* (David Owen; 2003) A poignant recounting of the demise of the Tasmanian tiger.

Best
Activities

It's not so much what's *in* Hobart that appeals to active types, it's what around the city: surf beaches, Kunanyi/Mt Wellington, the Derwent River and, of course, Tasmania's world-famous wilderness areas are all within easy reach. Cycling, mountain biking and bushwalking are *de rigueur* here: see the Greater Hobart Trails website (www.greaterhobarttrails.com.au) for details on dozens of options around the city.

PAPARWIN TANUPATARACHAI / GETTY IMAGES ©

Swimming & Surfing

Hobart's city beaches look inviting, especially at Bellerive and Sandy Bay, but the water here tends to get a bit soupy. For a safe, clean swim, you'll be better off heading further south to the beaches at **Kingston** and **Blackmans Bay**. Or smash out some laps at the Hobart Aquatic Centre.

The most reliable local surfing spots near Hobart are **Clifton Beach** and **Goats Beach**, en route to South Arm – about 30km and 35km from Hobart respectively. Note that Goats is unpatrolled and has a strong longshore drift.

Activities

Mt Wellington Descent Bombard down Mt Wellington on a mountain bike. (p120)

Roaring 40s Kayaking Paddle the Battery Point foreshore, Hobart wharves and beyond. (p102)

Kunanyi/Mt Wellington Tackle a steep mountainside track on Hobart's resident peak. (p119)

Hobart Bike Hire Get two wheels underneath you and explore the city, or pedal the 20km north to MONA along a Intercity Cycleway. (p56)

Hobart Aquatic Centre Cool off with a splash at Hobart's excellent swim centre. (p80)

☑ Top Tips

Hobart isn't big on bike lanes, but there's a terrific cycling path running from the Cenotaph near the waterfront all the way north to MONA, following an old railway line. It's called the **Intercity Cycleway**, and is about 20km one-way; see www.greaterhobarttrails.com.au/track/intercity-cycleway for details.

Best
Shopping

No-one has ever said, 'I'm off to Hobart with the express purpose of doing some serious shopping – can't wait!'. That said, there are some fabulous markets here, plus quirky city shops, purveyors of fine food and drink, quality bookshops, outdoor stores aplenty, and some brilliant galleries around Salamanca Place.

GRANT DIXON / GETTY IMAGES ©

Best Speciality Shops

Fullers Bookshop
Time is meaningless in Hobart's best bookshop: step inside then emerge pleasantly bewildered, three hours later. (p40)

Cool Wine The best of Tasmania's super cool-climate wines (and beer, whisky, gin, cider ...). (p27)

Wursthaus Stock up on gourmet goodies at this excellent deli, just off Salamanca Place. (p69)

Tommy Gun Records Thumb through racks of vinyl and tune in to the sounds of the city. (p27)

State Cinema Bookstore Browse arty titles adjacent to North Hobart's State Cinema. (p87)

Handmark Gallery
Hand-made, 100% Tasmanian arts and crafts on Salamanca Place: Handmark sets the benchmark. (p67)

Kathmandu Gear-up for your imminent Tasmanian wilderness adventure. (p69)

Best Markets

Salamanca Market Hobart's famous street market happens every Saturday morning, rain or shine. (p66)

Farm Gate Market Upstart Sunday-morning food-and-drink market on Bathurst St in the city. (p34)

Street Eats @ Franko Ebullient Friday-night food, drinks and entertainment at Franklin Sq in the city centre. (p34)

☑ Top Tips

▶ Hiking, camping, fishing and skiing is big business here: outdoors shops cluster around the Elizabeth St/Bathurst St intersection, or head to Kathmandu in Salamanca Square.

▶ Hobart is chilly in winter (and, truth be told, at times in spring, autumn and summer): it follows that the bookshops here are pretty good! Get yourself something good to leaf through by an open fire.

Best
With The Kids

Hobart is an outdoorsy kinda town, and despite its rep for being cold (yes, it is), it's the second driest capital city in Australia. There's lots to do that's free, good museums for when it does rain, and plenty of active things to do around town.

GRANT DIXON / GETTY IMAGES ©

Best Rainy-day Distractions

Tasmanian Museum & Art Gallery Check out some Aboriginal history, get the low-down on the elusive Tasmanian tiger and ogle some shiny stones – what's not to like? Pick up a 'Discovery Backpack' or a 'Museum Toolkit' from the front desk to assist the littl'uns with their explorations and learnings. (p48)

Maritime Museum of Tasmania Shipwrecks, whaling, yachts, rusty anchors – if there's anything uninteresting at this museum, let us know. (p56; pictured above right)

Mawson's Huts Replica Museum *Brrr,* Antarctica! Give the little blighters a concept of true hardship and see if their behaviour improves. (p56)

Best Entertainment

Rektango The free Friday-night Rektango music event in the courtyard at the Salamanca Arts Centre is a family-friendly affair: wear your dancin' shoes. (p47)

Salamanca Market The street performers, buskers and visual smorgasbord of Saturday's Salamanca Market captivate kids of all ages. (p66)

Waterfront There's always something going on down on the Hobart waterfront – fishing boats chugging in and out of Victoria Dock, yachts tacking in Sullivans Cove – and you can feed the tribe on a budget at the floating fish punts

on Constitution Dock (seagulls guaranteed). (p42)

☑ **Top Tips**

▶ Pick up the free *LetsGoKids* magazine (www. letsgokids.com.au) at the Hobart Visitor Information Centre for activity ideas.

▶ Kids under five travel free on Metro Tasmania public buses; over-fives receive discounted fares (around 50% off).

▶ If you're in need of a romantic dinner for two, contact the **Mobile Nanny Service** (📞 0437 504 064, 03 6273 3773; www. mobilenannyservice. com.au).

Best **Tours**

Taking a guided tour is a terrific way to get under Hobart's skin, be it with a historic, foodie, boozy or active focus. And if you don't have your own transport, taking a tour is the only way to access some key sights in and around Hobart, including Kunanyi/Mt Wellington.

GRANT DIXON / GETTY IMAGES ©

Best Walking Tours

Hobart Historic Tours
Entertaining strolls around the old town and Battery Point. Pub tours also available. (p31)

Ghost Tours of Hobart & Battery Point There are more than a few skeletons rattling in Hobart's closet. (p102)

Hobart Comedy Tours Walk around Franklin Sq in the city centre and have a laugh at Hobart's expense. (p31)

Best Food & Drink Tours

Gourmania Excellent walking tours around Hobart and Salamanca Place, stopping to taste as often as possible. (p57)

Tasmanian Whisky Tours Whisky, wine, beer and cider: day trips from the waterfront to sample the best drops. (p57; Lark Distillery, p64, pictured above right)

Best Sightseeing

Pennicott Wilderness Journeys Outstanding boat trips to some gorgeous southern coastal spots. The 'Tasmanian Seafood Seduction' tour is a hit with foodies. (p56)

Red Decker If you're short on time, this big red hop-on/hop-off bus is the way to see the sights pronto. (p58)

Tours Tasmania Day trips around Hobart, including the Port Arthur Historic Site and a trip up Kunanyi/Mt Wellington. (p58)

☑ Top Tips

▶ River cruises (including the ferry to MONA) set sail from the Hobart waterfront.

▶ Most bus tours depart from the Hobart Visitor Information Centre at the lower end of Elizabeth St.

▶ Most tours run daily during summer (December to February), but schedules and prices vary with the season and demand. Call in advance to confirm.

Hobart Historic Tours
Boat tours on the river: Hobart sure does look pretty from the water! (p31)

Best
For Free

You needn't break the bank on a trip to Hobart: there are plenty of free markets and indoor/outdoor activities around town that won't shred the contents of your wallet. Our best advice is to sight-see under your own steam: it's a compact town by Australian standards, with the city centre, waterfront, Salamanca Place and Battery Point all withing striding distance of one another. Even North Hobart is walkable.

PETER PTSCHELINZER / GETTY IMAGES ©

Best Outdoors

Royal Tasmanian Botanical Gardens
We're not sure that Queen Liz comes here too often, but these lovely gardens are a top spot for a stroll. (p79)

Kunanyi/Mt Wellington
'The mountain' is free but delivers in spades: drive to the summit, scan the far horizons, maybe throw a few snowballs... (p119)

Waterfront
Ship-spotters rejoice! Hobart's harbour is a busy hub of comings and goings: yachts, fishing boats, cruise ships, Antarctic supply vessels... (p52)

Battery Point
Get a dose of Hobart history with a self-guided wander around this super-charming historic enclave. (p94)

Best Indoors

Tasmanian Museum & Art Gallery
TMAG is free to all comers – what a noble piece of state government magnanimity! (p48)

Hobart Real Tennis Club
Visit this historic hall on Davey St and watch some free 'real' tennis (like the outdoor version, but with zany quirks). (p29)

Parliament House
Tours of Hobart's stately waterfront Parliament House are free (not when parliament is sitting, unfortunately). (p52)

Gasworks Cellar Door
Wander through the rooms of this interesting wine centre and learn all about Tasmania's booming booze industry. (p30)

Best Markets

Salamanca Market
Hobart's famous street market is a wandering and people-watching hotspot. Don't even think about doing anything else on a Saturday morning. (p66)

Farm Gate Market
You'll probably end up buying some food here (thus it's not *technically* free), but you can't put a price on atmosphere and good vibes. (p34)

Street Eats @ Franko
Tune in to some free live music at this engaging Friday-night food mart in Franklin Sq. (p34)

Best
Festivals

Best In Summer

Taste of Tasmania On either side of New Year's Eve, this week-long harbourside event is a celebration of Tassie's gastronomic prowess (pictured right). The seafood, wines and cheeses are predictably fab, or branch out into mushrooms, truffles, raspberries... Stalls are a who's-who of the Hobart restaurant scene. Live music, too. Just brilliant. (www.thetasteoftasmania.com.au; ☉Dec & Jan)

Hobart International As a prelude to the Australian Open tennis championship in Melbourne later in January, the Hobart International draws plenty of big-name players (just the ladies) for a week-long tournament. (p134)

Sydney to Hobart Yacht Race Maxi-yachts competing in the world's most gruelling open-ocean race start arriving in Hobart around 29 December – just in time for New Year's

Eve! (Yachties sure can party.) (p59)

MONA FOMA MONA's Festival of Music & Arts is a highlight of Hobart's busy January party schedule. Classy acts of all genres and persuasions. (p90)

Hobart BeerFest More than 200 brews from around Australia and the world, with brewing classes and lots of opportunities for waterfront snacking, foot tapping and imbibing. (www.hobart.beerfestivals.com.au; ☉Jan)

Falls Festival The Tasmanian version of the Victorian rock festival is a winner! Three nights and four days of live Oz and international tunes (Paul Kelly, Bloc Party, Cold War Kids, Alt J) at Marion Bay, an hour east of Hobart. (www.fallsfestival.com.au; ☉29 Dec-1 Jan)

Ten Days on the Island Tasmania's premier cultural festival is a biennial event (odd-numbered years), closing out the summer festival season

with fine Tasmanian arts, music and culture. Myriad concerts, exhibitions, workshops and dance, film and theatre happenings. (www.tendays.org.au; ☉Mar)

Best In Winter

Dark MOFO This noir little number broods in the low light of June's winter solstice. Expect edgy performances, epic installations, poetry, film, bonfires, red wine and feasting, all mainlining Tasmania's gothic blood flow. (p90)

Festival of Voices Sing to keep the winter chills at bay during this quirky vocal festival, featuring performances, workshops, cabaret and choirs at venues around town. (www.festivalofvoices.com; ☉Jul)

Survival Guide

Survival Guide

Before You Go

....

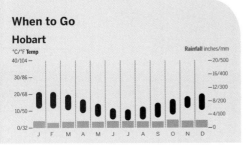

When to Go

Hobart

°C/°F **Temp**   **Rainfall** inches/mm

40/104 —   — 20/500

30/86 —   — 16/400

20/68 —   — 12/300

10/50 —   — 8/200

0/32 —   — 4/100

        J F M A M J J A S O N D   — 0

➡ **Summer (Dec–Feb)**
cell Peak tourist season:
the weather is at its
warmest and big-ticket
events keep the hordes
entertained.

➡ **Autumn (Mar–May)**
Atmospheric autumn
leaves and smoky eve-
nings. Easter is busy (late
March or early April) –
book beds ahead.

➡ **Winter (Jun–Aug)**
Sure, it's cold, but there's
snow on Kunanyi/Mt
Wellington and the Dark
MOFO festival warms
Hobart's collective soul.

➡ **Spring (Sep–Nov)**
Spring brings flower
blooms and optimism –
and it's the perfect time
to sidestep the crowds.

Book Your Stay

➡ Hobart has plenty of
budget hostels and pubs
offering accommodation,
some salubrious, some
not so much...

➡ Like the rest of Tasma-
nia, midrange accommo-
dation here isn't exactly a
bargain (B&Bs and motels,
mostly).

➡ Top-end accommoda-
tion, conversely, can be
quite reasonable. If your
budget stretches beyond
$250 per night, you can
afford something quite
special: designer hotels,
historic guesthouses
and mod waterside
apartments.

➡ Booking ahead is always
a good idea, regardless of
season.

Useful Websites

Discover Tasmania
(www.discovertasmania.
com.au) Comprehensive
listings in Hobart and
across the state.

Hobart & Beyond (www.hobartandbeyond.com) Select Hobart listings.

Lonely Planet (www.lonelyplanet.com/australia/tasmania/hobart/hotels) Recommendations and bookings.

Best Budget

Montacute (www.montacute.com.au) Assess the aesthetics of the other flashpackers in Hobart's best hostel.

The Nook (www.thenookbackpackers.com.au) Hobart's newest hostel-in-a-converted-pub makes a good job of it.

Alabama Hotel (www.alabamahobart.com.au) Fab retro pub conversion in the city centre.

Cassie Back-packers (www.brunswickhotelhobart.com.au) Upstairs at the venerable old Brunswick Hotel is one of Hobart's better hostels.

Hobart Central YHA (www.yha.com.au) A predictably clean, tidy and well-managed city YHA.

Hobart's Accommodation & Hostel (www.hobarthostel.com)

Above-board backpackers in a converted pub on the city fringe.

Best Midrange

Astor Private Hotel (www.astorprivatehotel.com.au) Endearing old hotel in the city with boundless charm.

Quayle Terrace (www.quayleterrace.com.au) Renovated Battery Point terrace house, perfect for a small family.

Old Woolstore Apartment Hotel (www.oldwoolstore.com.au) Play international CEO at these slick waterside apartments.

Apartments on Star (www.apartmentsonstar.com.au) Nifty contemporary apartments in an excellent Sandy bay location.

Quest Savoy (www.questapartments.com.au) Super-duper modern studios in a converted downtown bank.

Altamont House (www.airbnb.com.au/rooms/5353814) A plush double suite in a gorgeous 1854 stone-and-slate house in West Hobart.

Best Top End

Grande Vue Private Hotel (www.grandevuehotel.com.au) The best B&B in the city has gorgeous river and mountain views.

Islington (www.islingtonhotel.com) Opulent homestead in atmospheric South Hobart.

Henry Jones Art Hotel (www.thehenryjones.com) Boutique waterside warehouse conversion hung with gorgeous art.

Somerset on the Pier (www.somerset.com) You want water views with that? Fab apartments in Elizabeth St Pier.

Salamanca Wharf Hotel (www.salamancawharfhotel.com) Slick new one-bedroom apartments just east of Salamanca Place.

Sullivans Cove Apartments (www.sullivanscoveapartments.com.au) Sassy boutique apartments, dotted around the Hobart waterfront in five locations.

Arriving in Hobart

Hobart Airport

In an irony that doesn't elude the locals, Hobart's 'international' **airport** (☑ 03 6216 1600; www.hobartairport.com.au; Strachan St, Cambridge) has only domestic flights (perhaps we should commend the optimism?). The airport is at Cambridge, 19km east of the city.

➡ Services are operated by **Qantas** (www.qantas.com.au), **Virgin Australia** (www.virginaustralia.com.au), **Jetstar** (www.jetstar.com.au) and **Tiger Air** (www.tigerair.com.au), with direct flights from Melbourne, Sydney, Brisbane and sometimes Canberra.

➡ There's no public transport to Hobart Airport.

➡ Many visitors to Hobart rent a car: rental desks proliferate in the airport terminal.

➡ A taxi into the city will cost around $50 and take about 20 minutes.

➡ Pre-booked **Hobart Airporter** (☑ 1300 385 511; www.airporterhobart.com.au; one-way adult/ child $19/14, return $35/25) shuttle buses meet every flight and can deliver you door-to-door.

Devonport Ferry Terminal

If you're arriving by ferry from Melbourne aboard the **Spirit of Tasmania** (☑ 03 6421 7209, 1800 634 906; www.spiritoftasmania.com.au), the big red boat spits you out in Devonport on Tasmania's northwest coast. It's a 3¼-hour drive from here to Hobart.

Bus Stations

There are two main intrastate bus companies operating here – **Redline Coaches** (☑ 1300 360 000; www.redlinecoaches.com.au; 230 Liverpool St, Hobart; ☺ 8am-6pm) and **Tassielink** (☑ 1300 300 520; www.tassielink.com.au; 64 Brisbane St, Hobart).

➡ Redline buses arrive/ depart from their office at 230 Liverpool St.

➡ Tassielink buses leave Hobart from 64 Brisbane St (a former office) and a temporary stop on Elizabeth St, across the road from the Hobart Visitor Information Centre (a permanent bus depot is being planned – call or check the website for updates).

➡ Check online for fares, routes and timetables.

Main Access Roads

➡ From the airport, east coast or Tasman Peninsula, the approach to the city is via the Tasman Bridge (A3).

➡ From the north (eg from the car ferry), the view of the city from the high-point of the Brooker Hwy (Hwy 1) will give you a good sense of the lay of the land.

➡ From the south, the approach is via the steep Southern Outlet (A6) road which spits you out in South Hobart.

Getting Around

Bicycle

There are a number of bike-hire outlets around the city: it's a handy, affordable option if the weather is looking good and you don't mind sweating it out on a hill or three.

Bus

The local bus network is operated by **Metro Tasmania** (☑13 22 01; www. metrotas.com.au), which is reliable but infrequent outside of business hours.

➡ The **Metro Shop** (22 Elizabeth St, Hobart; ◷8am-6pm Mon-Fri, 9.30am-2pm Sat) handles ticketing and enquiries: most buses depart from this section of Elizabeth St, or from nearby Franklin Sq.

➡ One-way cash ticket prices vary with the number of zones travelled: one zone $3.30, two zones $4.60, or all zones $6.90. Fares into non-urban zones are additional to these costs.

➡ Buy a rechargeable **Greencard** in store or online from the Metro Shop for a 20% discount on regular fares.

➡ One-way tickets can be bought from the Metro Shop, the driver (exact change required), or ticket agents (newsagents and post offices).

Car & Motorcycle

This is the best way to explore Hobart. There are no toll roads here, but the CBD's one-way system can be a bit mind-boggling.

Rental

The big-boy rental firms have airport desks and city offices. Cheaper local firms offer daily rental rates from as low as $30. Note that some companies don't allow you to take their cars onto Bruny Island: ask when you book.

Parking

Timed, metered parking predominates in the CBD and tourist areas such as Salamanca Place and the waterfront. Parking inspectors here have a sixth sense – don't even think about overstaying! For longer-term parking, large CBD car parks (clearly signposted) offer reasonable rates.

Taxi

Hobart's taxi services pick up the slack from the bus network, with ranks in key areas such as Salamanca Place, North Hobart and the CBD. Or you can book one over the phone or online.

➡ **131008 Hobart** (☑13 10 08; www.131008hobart.com) Standard taxis.

➡ **Maxi-Taxi Services** (☑13 32 22; www.hobart maxitaxi.com.au) Wheelchair-accessible vehicles, and taxis for groups.

➡ **Yellow Cab Co** (☑13 19 24; hobart.yellowcab.com.au) Standard cabs (not all of which are yellow).

➡ **Uber** (www.uber.com) also operates in Hobart.

Walking

➡ Downtown Hobart is a compact area: if you're only here for a short time and aren't exploring beyond the CBD, Battery Point and waterfront, walking is a fine option.

➡ If staying in West or North Hobart, Sandy Bay or beyond, you may be in for a long trudge back to your bed. Do some planning before you decide to rely on the soles of your feet to get around.

Essential Information

Business Hours

Banks 9.30am–4pm Monday to Thursday, to 5pm Friday

Cafes 7.30am–4pm

Post Offices 9am–5pm Monday to Friday; some open Saturday morning

Pubs & Bars 11am–11pm daily (bars often close later)

Restaurants lunch noon–2pm and dinner 6pm–8.30pm

Shops 9am–5pm Monday to Friday, 9am–noon or 5pm Saturday, late-night city shopping to 8pm Friday

Discount Cards

➡ **iVenture Card** (📞02 9263 1100; www. iventurecard.com/au/ tasmania; 3-/5-/7-ticket pass adult $109/159/199, child $69/99/109) Flexible combo passes to a selection of the main tourist lures around Hobart and the rest of Tasmania.

Electricity

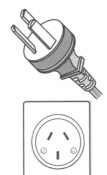

Type I
230V/50Hz

Emergency

➡ Dial 📞000 for police, fire and ambulance emergencies.

➡ **Hobart Police Station** (📞03 6230 2111, non-emergency assistance 13 14 44; www.police.tas.gov.au; 43 Liverpool St, Hobart; ⏱24hr) Hobart's main cop shop.

Insurance

➡ A good travel insurance policy covering theft, loss and medical problems is essential.

➡ Some policies specifically exclude designated 'dangerous activities' such as scuba diving, surfing and even bushwalking: ensure the policy you choose fully covers you for your activity of choice, and covers ambulances and emergency medical evacuations by air.

➡ Worldwide travel insurance is available at www. lonelyplanet.com/travel-insurance. You can buy, extend and claim online any time – even if you're already on the road.

Internet Access

➡ Wireless access is fast becoming a given in most Hobart accommodation. If access is not totally free, you might still get a certain amount of data gratis, then pay-per-use after that.

➡ See www.freewifi.tas. gov.au for free government-sponsored wi-fi locations around the city.

➡ Hobart cafes and pubs have been slow to adopt free wi-fi for customers, though you can find it (you might have to ask).

➡ **State Library of Tasmania** (📞03 6165 5597; www.linc.tas.gov.au; 91 Murray St, Hobart; ⏱9.30am-6pm Mon-Thu, to 8pm Fri, to 2pm Sat) Free pre-booked internet terminals.

LGBTIQ Travellers

It wasn't always the case, but Tasmania

is now considered by LGBTIQ rights groups to have greater equality in criminal law for homosexual and heterosexual people than most other Australian states. But beyond the law, a lack of discrimination outside of urban centres should never be assumed.

➡ Hobart has one gay bar – **Flamingos Dance Bar** (☏03 6294 6173; www.facebook.com/flamingosdancebar; 201 Liverpool St, Hobart; ⏰10pm-late Fri & Sat) – but most urban venues are open-minded.

➡ **Gay Tasmania** (www.gaytasmania.com.au) Accommodation and travel info.

➡ **TasPride** (www.taspride.com) Info on upcoming events, including November's annual TasPride Festival.

Media

➡ *Warp* (www.warpmagazine.com.au) Tasmania's free music and arts street press, covering the whole state.

➡ *The Mercury* (www.themercury.com.au) Local newspaper, covering Hobart and the south.

➡ *Tasmania 40° South* (www.fortysouth.com.au)

An excellent quarterly magazine with food, travel and wildlife stories.

Mobile Phones

➡ European phones will work on Australia's network, but most American or Japanese phones will not.

➡ Use global roaming or buy a local SIM card with a prepaid account you can top-up.

➡ Local numbers with the prefix 04 belong to mobile phones.

➡ Reception is good throughout Hobart CBD and suburbs.

Money

The major banks all have branches and ATMs around the Elizabeth St Mall. There are also ATMs around Salamanca Place.

➡ **ATMs** Hobart is flush with ATMs, from the airport to the city centre and suburban shopping strips. You'll also sometimes find a multicard ATM in the local grocery store, pub or petrol station.

➡ **Credit Cards** Credit cards such as MasterCard and Visa are widely accepted for most accommodation

and services, and a credit card is essential to hire a car. Diners Club and American Express cards are not as widely accepted.

➡ **Currency** The Australian dollar (AUD) comprises 100 cents. There are 5c, 10c, 20c, 50c, $1 and $2 coins, and $5, $10, $20, $50 and $100 notes.

➡ **Debit Cards** For international travellers, debit cards connected to the international banking networks – Cirrus, Maestro, Plus and Eurocard – will work fine in Hobart ATMs. Expect substantial fees. A better option may be prepaid debit cards (such as MasterCard and Travelex 'Cash Passport' cards) with set withdrawal fees and a balance you can top up from your bank account while on the road.

➡ **Eftpos** Almost all retail outlets have Eftpos, which allows you to pay for purchases electronically by card without a fee.

➡ **Tipping** Common in Australia in many situations, but certainly not mandatory. In restaurants and upmarket cafes, tip 10% of the bill if the service warrants it.

Taxes & Refunds

➡ Australia has a flat 10% tax on all goods and services (GST), included in quoted/shelf prices.

➡ A refund is sometimes possible under the Tourist Refund Scheme (TRS); see www.border. gov.au/trav/ente/tour/ are-you-a-traveller.

Public Holidays

Hobartians observe the following public holidays:

➡ **New Year's Day**
1 January

➡ **Australia Day**
26 January

➡ **Hobart Regatta Day**
2nd Monday in February

➡ **Eight Hour Day**
2nd Monday in March

➡ **Easter** March/April (Good Friday to Easter Tuesday inclusive)

➡ **Anzac Day** 25 April

➡ **Queen's Birthday**
2nd Monday in June

➡ **Hobart Show**
3rd Thursday in October

➡ **Christmas Day**
25 December

➡ **Boxing Day**
26 December

School Holidays

➡ The Christmas/summer school-holiday season runs from mid-December to late January.

➡ Three shorter school holiday periods occur during the year: roughly from early to mid-April, late June to mid-July, and late September to early October.

Safe Travel

➡ Hobart is just as safe as any other Australian capital city: common sense will get you by.

➡ Mt Wellington looks close enough to be a Hobart suburb…but the weather here can change rapidly. If you're

bushwalking or biking, check the forecasts and be prepared for anything.

➡ Hobart has always been a hard-drinking town: late night on the waterfront can get a bit unpleasant from time to time.

Toilets

➡ Toilets in Hobart are sit-down Western style.

➡ There aren't too many public toilets in central Hobart: try Salamanca Sq, or head into a pub.

➡ Alternatively, many parks and playgrounds around the suburbs have public toilets; see www. toiletmap.gov.au for locations.

Tourist Information

➡ **Hobart Visitor Information Centre** (☑ 03 6238 4222; www. hobarttravelcentre.com.au; cnr Davey & Elizabeth Sts, Hobart; ⏰ 9am-5pm) Poised perfectly between the CBD and the waterfront. Information, maps and state-wide tour, transport and accommodation bookings.

➡ **Hobart City Council** (☑ 03 6238 2711; www. hobartcity.com.au) City-council information: parks, transport, events and recreation.

Money-Saving Tips

➡ Central Hobart and the waterfront area are compact enough to walk around: save on taxi fares and hoof it instead.

➡ If you're planning on catching a lot of buses, buy a **Greencard** from **Metro Tasmania** (☑ 13 22 01; www.metrotas.com.au) for 20% off regular fares.

➡ **Parks & Wildlife Service** (☎1300 827 727; www.parks.tas.gov.au; 134 Macquarie St, Hobart; ⏰9am-5pm Mon-Fri) For national parks info; inside the Service Tasmania office.

➡ **Wilderness Society Office** (☎03 6224 1550; www.wilderness.org.au; 130 Davey St, Hobart; ⏰9am-5pm Mon-Fri) Info on conservation in Tasmania's wilderness areas.

➡ **Discover Tasmania** (www.discovertasmania.com. au) A statewide, catch-all info repository.

Travellers with Disabilities

➡ In Hobart, an increasing number of accommodation providers and key attractions have access for those with limited mobility, and tour operators often have the appropriate facilities: call ahead to confirm.

➡ Download Lonely Planet's free Accessible Travel guide from http://lptravel.to/ AccessibleTravel.

➡ Also check out the *Hobart CBD Mobility Map* from the Hobart Visitor Information Centre.

Dos & Don'ts

Although largely informal in their everyday dealings, Hobartians do observe some (unspoken) rules of etiquette.

➡ **Greetings** Shake hands with men, women and children when meeting for the first time and when saying goodbye. Female friends are often greeted with a single kiss on the cheek.

➡ **Invitations** If you're invited to someone's house for a BBQ or dinner, don't turn up empty handed: bring a bottle of wine or some beers.

➡ **Shouting** No, not yelling. 'Shouting' at the bar means buying a round of drinks: if someone buys you one, don't leave without buying them one too.

Visas

All visitors to Australia, and thus Tasmania, need a visa. Apply online through the Department of Immigration & Border Protection (www.border. gov.au).

eVisitor (651)

➡ Many European passport holders are eligible for a free eVisitor visa, allowing stays in Australia for up to three months within a 12-month period.

➡ eVisitor visas must be applied for online. They are electronically stored and linked to individual passport numbers, so no stamp in your passport is required.

➡ It's advisable to apply at least 14 days prior to the proposed date of travel to Australia.

Electronic Travel Authority (ETA; 601)

➡ Passport holders from the European countries eligible for eVisitor visas, plus passport holders from Brunei, Canada, Hong Kong, Japan, Malaysia, Singapore, South Korea and the USA, can apply for either a visitor ETA or business ETA.

➡ ETAs are valid for 12 months, with stays of up to three months on each visit.

➡ ETA visas cost $20.

Behind the Scenes

Send Us Your Feedback

We love to hear from travellers – your comments help make our books better. We read every word, and we guarantee that your feedback goes straight to the authors. Visit **lonelyplanet.com/contact** to submit your updates and suggestions.

Note: We may edit, reproduce and incorporate your comments in Lonely Planet products such as guidebooks, websites and digital products, so let us know if you don't want your comments reproduced or your name acknowledged. For a copy of our privacy policy visit lonelyplanet.com/privacy.

Charles' Thanks

Huge thanks to Tasmin for the gig, and to all the helpful souls I met on the road in Tasmania who flew through my questions with the greatest of ease. Biggest thanks of all to Meg, who held the increasingly chaotic fort while I was busy scooting around in the sunshine ('Where's daddy?') – and made sure that Ione, Remy, Liv and Reuben were fed, watered, schooled, tucked-in and read-to.

Acknowledgements

Climate map data adapted from Peel MC, Finlayson BL & McMahon TA (2007) 'Updated World Map of the Köppen-Geiger Climate Classification', Hydrology and Earth System Sciences, 11, 163344.

Cover photograph: Cray fishing boats, Hobart; Grant Dixon/Getty ©

Contents photograph: Kunanyi/Mt Wellington; boripan chatree/Shutterstock ©

This Book

This 1st edition of Lonely Planet's *Pocket Hobart* guidebook was researched and written by Charles Rawlings-Way. This guidebook was produced by the following:

Destination Editor
Tasmin Waby

Product Editor
Hannah Cartmel

Senior Cartographer
Julie Sheridan

Book Designer
Wibowo Rusli

Assisting Editors
Bruce Evans, Catherine Naghten, Saralinda Turner

Cover Researcher
Campbell McKenzie

Thanks to Jennifer Carey, Ian Cartmel, Daniel Corbett, Joel Cotterell, Melanie Dankel, Liz Heynes, Claire Naylor, Rachel Rawling, Tony Wheeler, Tracy Whitmey, Polly Whittington

Index

Our Writer

Charles Rawlings-Way

Charles is a veteran travel writer who has penned 30-something titles for Lonely Planet – including guides to Singapore, Toronto, Sydney, Tasmania, New Zealand, the South Pacific and Australia – and numerous articles. After dabbling in the dark arts of architecture, cartography, project management and busking for some years, Charles hit the road for LP in 2005 and hasn't stopped travelling since.

Published by Lonely Planet Global Limited
CRN 554153
1st edition – November 2017
ISBN 978 1 78657 701 6
© Lonely Planet 2017   Photographs © as indicated 2017
10 9 8 7 6 5 4 3 2 1
Printed in Singapore